OPPOSING VIEWPOINTS®

Sports and Athletes

Other Books of Related Interest

OPPOSING VIEWPOINTS®

Sports and Athletes

James D. Torr, *Book Editor*

Bruce Glassman, *Vice President*
Bonnie Szumski, *Publisher*
Helen Cothran, *Managing Editor*

OPPOSING
VIEWPOINTS®
SERIES

GREENHAVEN PRESS
An imprint of Thomson Gale, a part of The Thomson Corporation

THOMSON
────────✦────────™
GALE

Detroit • New York • San Francisco • San Diego • New Haven, Conn.
Waterville, Maine • London • Munich

LIBRARY OF CONGRESS CATALOGING-IN-PUBLICATION DATA

Sports and athletes : opposing viewpoints / James D. Torr, book editor.
   p. cm. — (Opposing viewpoints series)
  Includes bibliographical references and index.
  ISBN 0-7377-2244-4 (lib. : alk. paper) — ISBN 0-7377-2245-2 (pbk. : alk. paper)
   1. Sports. 2. Athletes. I. Torr, James D., 1974– . II. Opposing viewpoints series (Unnumbered)
  GV706.8.S6625 2005
  796—dc22   2004053924

Printed in the United States of America

"Congress shall make no law... abridging the freedom of speech, or of the press."

First Amendment to the U.S. Constitution

The basic foundation of our democracy is the First Amendment guarantee of freedom of expression. The Opposing Viewpoints Series is dedicated to the concept of this basic freedom and the idea that it is more important to practice it than to enshrine it.

Contents

Why Consider Opposing Viewpoints?

"The only way in which a human being can make some approach to knowing the whole of a subject is by hearing what can be said about it by persons of every variety of opinion and studying all modes in which it can be looked at by every character of mind. No wise man ever acquired his wisdom in any mode but this."

John Stuart Mill

In our media-intensive culture it is not difficult to find differing opinions. Thousands of newspapers and magazines and dozens of radio and television talk shows resound with differing points of view. The difficulty lies in deciding which opinion to agree with and which "experts" seem the most credible. The more inundated we become with differing opinions and claims, the more essential it is to hone critical reading and thinking skills to evaluate these ideas. Opposing Viewpoints books address this problem directly by presenting stimulating debates that can be used to enhance and teach these skills. The varied opinions contained in each book examine many different aspects of a single issue. While examining these conveniently edited opposing views, readers can develop critical thinking skills such as the ability to compare and contrast authors' credibility, facts, argumentation styles, use of persuasive techniques, and other stylistic tools. In short, the Opposing Viewpoints Series is an ideal way to attain the higher-level thinking and reading skills so essential in a culture of diverse and contradictory opinions.

In addition to providing a tool for critical thinking, Opposing Viewpoints books challenge readers to question their own strongly held opinions and assumptions. Most people form their opinions on the basis of upbringing, peer pressure, and personal, cultural, or professional bias. By reading carefully balanced opposing views, readers must directly confront new ideas as well as the opinions of those with whom they disagree. This is not to simplistically argue that everyone who reads opposing views will—or should—change his or her opinion. Instead, the series enhances readers' understanding of their own views by encouraging confrontation with opposing ideas. Careful examination of others' views can lead to the readers' understanding of the logical inconsistencies in their own opinions, perspective on why they hold an opinion, and the consideration of the possibility that their opinion requires further evaluation.

Evaluating Other Opinions

To ensure that this type of examination occurs, Opposing Viewpoints books present all types of opinions. Prominent spokespeople on different sides of each issue as well as well-known professionals from many disciplines challenge the reader. An additional goal of the series is to provide a forum for other, less known, or even unpopular viewpoints. The opinion of an ordinary person who has had to make the decision to cut off life support from a terminally ill relative, for example, may be just as valuable and provide just as much insight as a medical ethicist's professional opinion. The editors have two additional purposes in including these less known views. One, the editors encourage readers to respect others' opinions—even when not enhanced by professional credibility. It is only by reading or listening to and objectively evaluating others' ideas that one can determine whether they are worthy of consideration. Two, the inclusion of such viewpoints encourages the important critical thinking skill of objectively evaluating an author's credentials and bias. This evaluation will illuminate an author's reasons for taking a particular stance on an issue and will aid in readers' evaluation of the author's ideas.

It is our hope that these books will give readers a deeper understanding of the issues debated and an appreciation of the complexity of even seemingly simple issues when good and honest people disagree. This awareness is particularly important in a democratic society such as ours in which people enter into public debate to determine the common good. Those with whom one disagrees should not be regarded as enemies but rather as people whose views deserve careful examination and may shed light on one's own.

Thomas Jefferson once said that "difference of opinion leads to inquiry, and inquiry to truth." Jefferson, a broadly educated man, argued that "if a nation expects to be ignorant and free . . . it expects what never was and never will be." As individuals and as a nation, it is imperative that we consider the opinions of others and examine them with skill and discernment. The Opposing Viewpoints Series is intended to help readers achieve this goal.

David L. Bender and Bruno Leone,
Founders

Greenhaven Press anthologies primarily consist of previously published material taken from a variety of sources, including periodicals, books, scholarly journals, newspapers, government documents, and position papers from private and public organizations. These original sources are often edited for length and to ensure their accessibility for a young adult audience. The anthology editors also change the original titles of these works in order to clearly present the main thesis of each viewpoint and to explicitly indicate the opinion presented in the viewpoint. These alterations are made in consideration of both the reading and comprehension levels of a young adult audience. Every effort is made to ensure that Greenhaven Press accurately reflects the original intent of the authors included in this anthology.

Introduction

"We must reclaim responsibility for shaping organized sports' proper role in our society."
—*John R. Gerdy, author of the* All-American Addiction

Sports are a major part of American society. It is only partly in jest that the Super Bowl is sometimes referred to as an unofficial national holiday—after all, the number of Americans who watch the event is roughly the same as the number who usually vote for president. From learning how to hit a baseball or dribble a basketball as children, to rooting for the home team at a high school or college football game, to reading about millionaire professional athletes in the news, sports provide a set of cultural experiences that almost all Americans take part in at some point in their lives. The question of whether sports' increasing impact on American society is positive or negative is now the center of heated debate.

Many people feel that sports are a positive force in society, particularly for children. It may be a cliché, but the idea that "sports build character" is the primary reason that many parents encourage a love of sports in their children. Many parents hope to instill in their sons and daughters lessons about sportsmanship, discipline, and respect for authority. As physician Douglas B. McKeag writes, "Where else do you find daily challenges confronting children that concern ethics and values, leadership and character issues, failure and success, and yet take place in the protected arena of sports?"

In fact, the orderly format of sporting events—in which athletes compete under a clear and open set of rules in order to better themselves and each other—is sometimes held up as a model for how society should function. Historian Francis Trevelyan Miller writes that "baseball is democracy in action: in it all men are 'free and equal,' regardless of race, nationality, or creed. Every man is given the rightful opportunity to rise to the top on his own merits." Sports have played a major role in many minorities' efforts to achieve equality, the most famous example being black athlete Jackie Robinson's crossing of baseball's color barrier in 1947.

However, the sports world is far from perfect. In some ways, its problems mirror the problems of society as a whole. For example, racial and gender inequalities still exist in sports, despite decades of progress, just as in the rest of society. Likewise, there will always be incidents of cheating and scandal in sports, just as there is lawbreaking and scandal in real life.

Other sports problems stem from their incredible popularity. Most of the criticisms of children's sports, for example, center on the argument that parents, coaches, and athletes have all become too obsessed with sports and too focused on winning. Organizations such as the Positive Coaching Alliance have arisen to address this "win at all cost" mentality, which the alliance warns "creates a pressure filled environment for the kids and ultimately turns them away from sports."

The controversies surrounding college and professional sports have mostly to do with the fact that they have become very big business. Whether the issue is rising ticket prices, performance-enhancing drugs, sports betting, or the outrageous behavior of some high-paid athletes, the major theme in these controversies is the fame and wealth that is accorded to winners in today's professional sports world. Journalist John Solomon describes how these controversies remain unresolved in professional sports:

> The $10 billion [pro sports] industry is run by almost completely unregulated monopolies. . . . Pro sports' failings don't get the coverage they deserve in the press. The national sports media are frequently "league partners" or even franchise owners (Fox and Time Warner are good examples) rendering their journalism on the subject less than objective.

The biggest problem in the world of pro sports, according to Solomon, is that "fans have never been willing to use their ultimate leverage over owners and players: their butts. . . . It is an interesting paradox: the public has never been so angry, but sports have never been so popular."

In his book *Sports: The All-American Addiction*, John R. Gerdy laments that "an honest rational argument can be made that organized sports' overall influence within our culture has become more negative than positive." The viewpoints in *Opposing Viewpoints: Sports and Athletes* examine whether sports are having a positive or negative influence on society in the following chapters: Do Sports Benefit Children? Should College Sports Be Reformed? Is Discrimination a Problem in Sports? Is Drug Use a Problem in Sports? Whatever the merits and shortcomings of sports, Gerdy believes that the public should address this aspect of American culture and work to change it for the better:

> As much as I would like to forget about sports' problems and simply enjoy the games, I cannot. Sports' influence on our lives and culture is simply too great for such concerns to be swept under the rug. . . . It is time to reclaim sports in America.

CHAPTER 1

Do Sports Benefit Children?

Chapter Preface

Sports have enormous potential to benefit children. In addition to fitness and fun, sports also give children opportunities to learn the value of teamwork, discipline, and sportsmanship. As sports psychologist Shari Young Kuchenbecker writers in her book *Raising Winners*, "Sports have a lot of lessons to teach—some of them tough, some of them fun—but all of them valuable."

However, there are also potential downsides to children's sports. Injuries are a serious concern, and some evidence indicates that sports-related injuries are increasing among children. The emotional intensity of sports can also be traumatic for children. "I'm concerned that [the] character-building attributes of kids' sports have become overshadowed today by a culture that is more competitive, is less focused on fun, and produces more injuries" writes *Physician & Sportsmedicine* editor in chief Gordon O. Matheson. Matheson and other experts argue that the main emphasis of children's sports should be on fun and self-improvement rather than on winning.

Experts also agree that parents have the biggest influence on whether their children enjoy and benefit from sports. "Good sports parents realize that sport is a tool to teach your child about life," says volunteer soccer coach Sue Mak. Unfortunately, a major problem in children's sports is the bad behavior of parents at children's sports matches. Many games are marred by incidents of parents losing their tempers, berating their children for poor play, and engaging in shouting matches and even fistfights with coaches and other parents. In the most tragic and publicized example, in July 2000 a father beat the adult supervising his son's hockey practice to the point that he died from his injuries two days later. Such incidents point to the need for parents to take a step back and evaluate their role in their child's sports program.

Sports should be a positive experience for children. The viewpoints in the following chapter examine whether this is the case and offer suggestions on how to improve children's sports.

"Children should not be permitted to participate in structured youth sports programs as we currently know them until they reach the age of thirteen."

Organized Sports Do Not Benefit Children

John R. Gerdy

In the following viewpoint John R. Gerdy argues that adults are ruining children's sports. Gerdy maintains that in adult-run, organized youth sports, the focus is on skill development and winning, whereas in child-run, pick-up games, the emphasis is on fun. Without adult-enforced structure and rules, writes Gerdy, children's games are more inclusive and enjoyable for all participants. The author suggests that, rather than monitoring games, adults should not play any role at all in pre–high school children's sports. Gerdy is visiting professor of sports administration at Ohio University and the author of *Sports: The All-American Addiction*, from which this article is excerpted.

As you read, consider the following questions:
1. Why do children want to play sports, in Gerdy's opinion?
2. What example does the author use to illustrate the difference between pick-up games and organized sports?
3. What types of administrative tasks, currently handled by adults, does the author believe student athletes should be given responsibility for?

It is no secret that there are significant problems with organized youth sports programs. Incidences of parents screaming at nine-year-old children over a missed basket or a misplayed fly ball are commonplace. Youth-league umpires are regularly abused and increasingly attacked. Brawls have erupted after youth-league soccer games. Obviously something is wrong.

What is wrong with youth sports is the adults. Youth sports programs are no longer about meeting the educational, developmental, and recreational needs of children but rather about satisfying ego needs of adults. Adults have imposed their values and priorities about sports upon their children's games, from the organization of player drafts to the imposition of structure, organization, and rules to a disproportionate emphasis placed on winning. This, despite the fact that children, more than anything else, want to play sports, not to win, but simply to have fun. It is the adults who are destroying youth sports. That being the case, it is time to give youth sports back to the children.

Kids Know How to Make Sports Fun

But how will our children manage without adults supervising their athletic activities? Quite well, thank you! Studies contrasting spontaneous youth play versus youth sport organized by adults indicate that children, if left to their own devices, will successfully organize, administer, and manage their own games. They will choose sides and mediate disputes. They will set their own rules. In some cases, those rules may change from game to game. But they will be rules that work for the children. Children will handicap their games to ensure they are evenly matched, interesting, and fun. Such organizational, mediation, and interpersonal skills are valuable characteristics that children are not permitted to develop when they are forced by adults to play the "adult," supposedly *right*, way.

A perfect example of the stark difference between "pick-up" and "organized" adult-run youth games is the typical situation where there is one very superior athlete in a baseball game. In the "organized" game, the adult coach will have that child pitch. The child proceeds to dominate the game, striking out most of the batters he or she faces, while the children in the field stand like statues waiting to field a ball that has virtually no chance of being hit to them. By the end of the game, many players have never handled the ball. If left to their own devices, the children in the "pick-up" game will agree amongst themselves that the dominant player either not pitch or pitch with his or her opposite arm. In basketball, the dominant player may be allowed only a limited number of shots or may be required to shoot with his or her "off" hand.

Children make adjustments in their games to ensure that the game will be interesting and fun, and thus, continue. Their purpose in getting together to play is, after all, to have fun. If the game is not fun, children will quit playing and, if enough quit, the game will end. That being the case, they must work to make the game interesting and enough fun so everyone will want to continue to play. Without adult-enforced structure, rules, and expectations, there is nothing holding the game together other than the children actually wanting to play it. And what holds the game together is being involved and having fun. In short, the game would not exist if it were not fun. In youth leagues organized by adults, the adult-imposed goal of winning replaces the goal of maximizing fun and participation.

Another significant difference between these two types of games is the way in which the outcome of the game is treated. In adult-organized games, the result of the contest is recorded as a win or a loss, regardless of the closeness of the game or the performances of the individuals involved. In the pick-up game, while the result may be discussed on the walk home, it is usually considered insignificant and quickly forgotten as the children focus more on the actions of the individuals and the fun they had. Clearly, the children have their priorities straight regarding sports as it is the process (participation and having fun) rather than the end result that is most important.

De-organizing Children's Sports

How do we restructure youth sports programs to give the games back to the children? "De-organize" them. Children should not be permitted to participate in structured youth sports programs as we currently know them until they reach the age of thirteen. Prior to that, they should participate only in "de-organized" youth sports activities. In such "de-

Pressure from Parents and Coaches

Fun and fitness sounds like a promising combination. They are the goals of nearly all children when they first become involved in sports. Unfortunately, those goals can become obscured once some young athletes enter the world of competition for the first time. Too often they end up playing not for fun and fitness but to please the adults in their lives.

One group the young athletes seek to please is parents. Sports columnist Joan Ryan says that, despite our best intentions, there is a bit of the stage mom or dad in every parent, and "we cover it up under the guise of 'wanting the best for our children'". Too many parents see their children as a way to rekindle their own failed dreams of athletic glory or to enhance their own prestige or reputation within a community. They fail to provide their sons and daughters with the element most necessary to achieving athletic success: the ability to develop ambition on their own, separate and distinct from the ambitions of adults. Parents can help develop that ambition by focusing on basic athletic skills while their kids are under the age of ten, and by showing their kids how much they themselves enjoy sports.

As young athletes grow older, the process can become more complicated. The peer pressure of adolescence arrives, the level of competition increases, and the emotional and financial investments of parents can become deeper. Most important, a coach can emerge as a key influence. That is not always a positive development. When Nicolas Clark, a Little League Baseball player in Crown Point, Indiana, won a trophy in 1995 as a member of a championship team, he instead handed the trophy back to the league's board of directors. "The coaches treated me like scum," he said. "I don't want this". Clark's coaches had stood idly by as Clark's teammates taunted him relentlessly for his lack of skill. And when his mother complained to the coaches and said all her son wanted to do was have fun, she was informed that the game was about winning. If Nicolas wanted to have fun, he was advised to do so elsewhere.

Douglas T. Putnam, *Controversies of the Sports World*. Westport, CT: Greenwood Press, 1999.

20

organized" activities, no more than 25 percent of the playtime should be devoted to fundamental skill instruction. The remaining time should be turned over to the kids for them to play pick-up games . . . with no parental or adult involvement! Other than a safety official, adults should not be permitted to coach, instruct, or even watch. The real joy of youth sports comes from playing with friends, far from critiquing and criticizing adults. Leave the kids alone! Let them pick their own teams, make their own rules, and mediate their own disputes. The only rule that they must abide by is that everyone plays.

In other words, to make youth sports "about the kids," athletic activities should resemble "pick-up" games. In my childhood, we organized, scheduled, administered, and refereed our own games. We would meet at a designated time or simply go door to door to see who was interested in playing a game. For safety reasons, parents today are hesitant to allow their children to roam the neighborhood unsupervised, searching for a basketball game. Under this proposal, children would be provided a safe playing environment, but would be allowed to manage their own games and, as a result, begin to develop those personal skills—organization, conflict resolution, leadership, management, and mediation—that make participation in athletics valuable. Other than specific playing skills and techniques, children learn very little from adult-organized athletics. While adults may cringe at denying children their "expert" coaching advice, the fact is, children's interpersonal skills will develop more if they are left to manage their own games. Without adult supervision, the games will be closer, more interesting and, most important, more fun. It is time to get adults out of youth sports. It is time to let the kids have their games back.

Adult Domination of Children's Sports

But the games must be returned to the players at all levels of play. For example, why do coaches, from pee-wee leagues to the college level, insist on calling every play and dictating how every minute of every practice is spent? Why not provide the opportunity for a high school or college quarterback to think for himself and exhibit leadership and decision-making skills by calling his own plays? After all, we claim that sports builds those skills. Or, what would be so detrimental in allowing a player to develop and implement a practice schedule or even be responsible for making travel arrangements for a road trip? Before full-time, paid coaches became a fixture in college athletics, students organized and administered all aspects of their programs without adult supervision. Today, other than actually playing in the game, adults perform virtually every task associated with youth, high school, and college athletics.

What are the consequences of the domination of adults over games allegedly designed for young people? There is evidence that athletic participation may not be developing the leadership skills we have long claimed that it does. Again, according to William G. Bowen and James J. Shulman, while those who play college sports feel that leadership is important in their lives and felt this way before college,

> Surprisingly, this greater inclination toward leadership is not reflected very clearly in any measure of actual leadership that we can identify. . . . Overall, College and Beyond (term used to describe students in their study) graduates who were athletes (and who went on to earn advanced degrees) seem slightly less likely than other C&B graduates to work in public affairs. Former athletes are no more likely than other C&B graduates to provide leadership in the marketplace via service as CEOs. . . . It is not clear what accounts for this disjunction between the subjective importance attached to leadership by athletes and the actual pattern of leadership that is displayed. Perhaps part of the explanation is as simple as the tendency for any group to believe certain "mantras." One such mantra is that athletics teaches leadership. Reiteration of such beliefs may outrun their translation into actual conduct.

The fact is, if organized athletics is ever going to meet its promise of developing the leadership, organization, and decision-making skills of participants, parents, coaches, and administrators must place their egos on the shelf and give the children and young adults the freedom to exercise and develop those skills. Ultimately, what difference does it make whether a junior high school quarterback calls for a pass on a third and three situation when the coach would have preferred to call a draw play? Or, whether a basketball squad comes to a decision amongst themselves during a timeout to set up for a three-point shot rather than dumping the ball into the low post? We claim that sports is for the kids, yet they have absolutely no ownership of the activity because the adults are making every decision for them. It is no longer their game. We need to give it back to them.

> *"There's . . . a positive side to the increasing
> organization of kids' sports: the emergence
> of good coaches, more and more of them
> each year."*

Organized Sports Can Benefit Children

David Brooks

Journalist David Brooks is senior editor of the *Weekly Standard* and the author of *Bobos in Paradise: The New Upper Class and How They Got There*. In the following viewpoint he maintains that, despite the negative attention that some youth sports leagues have received, organized sports have the potential to build children's character and teach them valuable life lessons. According to Brooks, the most important contributors to youth sports are coaches. Good coaches, in the author's view, teach children not just how to play the game but also the importance of leadership, responsibility, hard work, loyalty, and honor.

As you read, consider the following questions:

1. What two reasons does the author give for why coaches are able to talk confidently about the importance of character?
2. In Brooks's opinion, what do good coaches emphasize more than winning?
3. What is the ultimate lesson good coaches offer, in the author's opinion?

L ike most middle-aged American fathers, I drive to work lamenting the decline of Western civilization—the erosion of standards, the lack of responsibility, the inability of morning disc jockeys to shut up. But something happened one morning last summer [2001] that lifted my spirits from gloomy to positively rosy. I dropped my two eldest kids off at John McCarthy's baseball camp in Washington, D.C.

There were 150 6- to 12-year-olds sitting on some wooden bleachers, their little baseball hats on their heads, their gloves in their laps, when McCarthy opened camp by outlining his priorities. The first was playing safe. "Safety is your responsibility. I will not tolerate unsafe behavior," he said with a stern authority that had the kids rapt. Then he talked about neatness—in 2001! He pulled forward one of his coaches. "Look how he wears his uniform. Neat. Shirt tucked in. You will wear your uniform properly and look sharp." Later he pulled out another coach. "Look at the way he shines his shoes. A good shoeshine is a foundation for everything else."

Then he started introducing his 30-odd assistant coaches, who were in a line behind him. Some were college players with impressive athletic and academic records. Others were high-school kids who started at McCarthy's camp when they were 8 or 9. McCarthy said of one young coach, "I always remembered him because he came up to me at the end of each day and said 'Thank you.' Politeness is important to me." McCarthy went on to describe how one coach had impressed him because he always made eye contact when he spoke. Another drew praise because he came early to help prepare the field.

McCarthy went down the line and asked each coach what book he was reading. Then he dared to talk about the difference between being a successful player—thinking, hustling, encouraging—and merely winning.

I left and headed off to my office feeling that something unusual had happened. Here was a man willing to stand up in front of an audience week after week and actually talk unironically about honor and character and saying thank you.

Coaches Help Build Children's Character

We've all heard plenty about the fascist coaches who have turned their youth teams into little professional academies for trophy accumulation. But there's also a positive side to the increasing organization of kids' sports: the emergence of good coaches, more and more of them each year. As I've reported other stories on college campuses, in high schools, and around neighborhoods, I've begun to notice something: Coaches have become the leading moral instructors in America today.

We no longer regard them as dumb ex-jocks with whistles around their necks. In fact, now our talk of coaches is infused with moral meaning. Notre Dame named a research institute the Center for Sport, Character, and Culture. David Maraniss wrote a best-selling book on Vince Lombardi called *When Pride Still Mattered*. Nobody makes movies about streetwise young priests the way they used to, but there are dozens of movies, such as *Remember the Titans*, in which the coach is the beacon of virtue.

And when you think about it, you realize there actually aren't that many professions in American life in which people feel that their job is to build character. Lord knows, neither Hollywood nor the music industry offers much instruction on how to build character. Many religious leaders seem so desperate to appear "with it" to young people that they don't dare impose high standards on children. Even schools don't talk much about character. They tend to treat kids as little brains who have to master certain skills and do well on certain tests. I get the impression that a lot of today's teachers would like to instill good values, but they don't want anybody to accuse them of being judgmental, or of imposing their personal values on someone else's kid.

But coaches are different. You rarely see a teacher tell a kid to tuck in his shirt and have some pride in his appearance, but coaches do it all the time. The best coaches still live by a code, and they make no apology for demanding that kids live up to it.

Leadership and Responsibility

Why do coaches talk so confidently about character when so many others are morally tongue-tied? First, they still command authority. The same kids who've decided it's cool to dismiss teachers or parents will still listen to a coach. Go into a high school and watch the dynamics of a classroom. Very often it's the rebel flouting authority who's the coolest. But then go into a locker room. Nobody wants to be around the guy

Personal Development Through Sports

Some of life's most important lessons can be learned in the safe, supervised environment of sports. Shy four-year-old Caitlin learned to stretch and curl (like the legs on a spider) with her gym classmates and discovered she had made seven new friends at the same time. Fourteen-year-old Trevor was having trouble focusing in school. Then he became inspired by a new basketball coach, worked hard, excelled, then transferred his new work ethic to academics and made honor roll the next quarter. Ten-year-old Angela had always been overshadowed by her older brothers' academic prowess, but joined an American Youth Soccer Organization (AYSO) soccer team on which her quick running at forward brought in goal after goal. The joy of victory was made especially sweet through the newly earned respect of her big brothers. Matthew's first loss in an important ice hockey competition at age nine was the ideal opportunity for this natural athlete to begin to understand that quality of play is more important than the score on the board.

Sports are practice for real life. There are things to be learned. Rules to play by. Goals. Setbacks. Progress. Nurtured through adult guidance, sports provide many rich early learning opportunities for developing maturity.

Participation in sports also develops real self-esteem. Watch a young athlete's genuine joy after mastering a tricky new shot on goal in soccer. Notice the radiant grin of the skater who lands a double axel or the kid making the three-point shot for the first time. And does anyone ever forget that first home run? Solid self-esteem earned through hard work grows by meeting challenges on the playing field. Mastery empowers and cannot be artificially duplicated, taken away, or forgotten.

Playing sports also gets kids off the couch and into exercising. Physical activity is fun and promotes lifelong health. Research shows that the more time a kid (or adult) watches TV, the more likely he or she is to be overweight and underachieve academically. Lifespan specialists say, "Live longer—stay active" and "Use it or lose it!" All sports provide opportunities to learn and improve no matter where or when you begin.

Shari Young Kuchenbecker, *Raising Winners*. New York: Random House, 2000.

scoffing in the back. Everybody admires the team players.

Second, sports involve suffering. Grade inflation being what it is, and the self-esteem ethic being what it is, lots of kids can go through school and other parts of their lives without ever having to deal with humiliating failure. Everybody is above average. But in sports there is no escaping failure. In baseball you strike out, you walk in a run, you drop a ball. And you don't confront failure in the privacy of a small conference room or on a confidential report card. It happens to you on the field, in front of everybody.

Brandon Sullivan, another young coach who gives baseball clinics in the Washington area, calls these events teachable moments. "There are more teachable moments in a game of baseball than in a month of school. There is so much loss and failure and having to deal with them."

If you listen to coaches talk, or if you read through some of their advice books, you'll notice a consistent echo of chivalry. They tend to be fanatical about assuming personal responsibility and not blaming others for bad breaks.

In his book *Leading with the Heart*, Mike Krzyzewski, coach of the Duke University basketball team, tells of a time when, as a cadet at West Point, he was walking down the sidewalk and somebody stepped in a puddle, splashing mud on his shoes. Seconds later, an upperclassman barked at him for being dirty. Krzyzewski's first impulse was to blame the guy who'd splashed him. But then he realized it was his fault. He should have turned around immediately to go clean up. That's a story he tells his players about accepting responsibility when bad luck happens.

Hard Work and Loyalty

The best coaches, the McCarthys and the Sullivans, don't emphasize winning as much as effort. They demand practice. They demand unselfishness. If Sullivan's team is winning by 15 runs and a player is goofing around in the dugout, that player's in big trouble because he's not respecting the game and he's not respecting the other team.

Coaches are also zealous about work and preparation. The typical coach was once the kid who didn't have as much talent as some of the others, but figured he could bull his way to the top through hard work. These guys are still at it, which is why so many of the best coaches are up nights studying game films, and are sweating through their clothes while pacing up and down the sidelines like madmen. In his book *Competitive Leadership*, Brian Billick, coach of the Baltimore Ravens, quotes the military strategist Carl von Clausewitz: "The personal physical exertion of leaders must not be overlooked. It is as important as any strategy or tactic." And what they expect from themselves they also expect from their players.

Finally, good coaches believe in loyalty. So many relationships in life are conditional. You can change jobs, switch parties, or leave neighborhoods. But the best coaches give the impression that team loyalty is inviolable. That's because, while the rest of us work with keyboards or machinery, coaches work with people. Their tools are individuals. They often feel fiercely protective of them.

My own kids sometimes have trouble with the rudimentary techniques of cleaning up their rooms. But during the weeks they are at Coach McCarthy's baseball clinic, you can see my eldest son and daughter out in the backyard polishing their cleats. When we found them some fluffy polishing mitts to help them do a better job, they were as happy as if they'd been given a new bat.

The ultimate lesson good coaches offer is that if you demand that people live up to a rigorous code of honor, they are excited by the challenge. Unless I'm mistaken, kids are quietly ecstatic to find authority they can respect, learn from, and admire.

Each week McCarthy opens his camp with straight-ahead homilies about kids whose families can't afford baseball camp, or kids who don't respect their gear or take the time to learn from players less gifted than they are. The campers sit on the stands during these sermons, their parents in a reverent semicircle behind them.

One day, I heard a mother ask her boy what he thought of Coach's speech that day. "Aw, parents love that kind of stuff," he said.

True enough. Sometimes, you can look at the parents' faces and see the tears welling up in their eyes.

> *"There is an overemphasis on sports in the black community, and too many black students are putting all their eggs in one basket."*

A Preoccupation with Sports Is Detrimental to Black Youth

John Hoberman

John Hoberman is the author of *Darwin's Athletes: How Sport Has Damaged Black America and Preserved the Myth of Race*. He argues in the following viewpoint that too many African American children have unrealistically high hopes of becoming professional athletes. Worse, writes Hoberman, too many black children believe that sports are one of their only possible routes to future success. Hoberman contends that the high proportion of blacks in professional sports leagues has perpetuated the belief that there are biologically significant differences between blacks and whites. The result, according to the author, is the myth that blacks are better than whites at physical activities and worse than whites at intellectual pursuits.

As you read, consider the following questions:

1. In the school described by R. Patrick Solomon, what types of behavior were viewed as "acting white" by black children?
2. What sociologist first promulgated the idea that black Americans are overinvested in sports, according to the author?
3. What percent of black boys between thirteen and eighteen believed they could support themselves as professional athletes, according to the study cited by Hoberman?

John Hoberman, "The Price of 'Black Dominance,'" *Society*, vol. 37, March 2000, p. 49. Copyright © 2000 by Transaction Publishers, Inc. Reproduced by permission.

The somber and determined face of a young black man stares out from a glossy magazine page while an equally resolute text lets us read his mind: "I can tolerate mistakes. But I cannot repeat them. I can grow." This, of course, is how point guards and wide receivers must think to survive in the tough games they play. Suddenly the attentive eye catches a glimpse of the dress shirt and tie that are just visible at the bottom of the page, and cognitive dissonance sets in. For this positive thinker does not work for the National Football League (NFL) or the National Basketball Association (NBA). "I work for J.P. Morgan." This black man competes in banking, not basketball.

Clever advertising ploys like this illustrate one kind of progress in our society's unofficial and haphazard campaign to eliminate racial stereotyping from public spaces. For this well-dressed (and well-integrated) man represents the new entrepreneurial alternative to more familiar racial images—the sullen faces of black athletes we have seen looking tough and sweaty for the cameras that serve the marketing interests of athletic shoe companies and other sponsors. Any attentive observer of our advertising conventions will have noticed that basketballs and naked muscled torsos have long served as de facto signifiers of black masculinity for an audience that now includes almost anyone on earth. A few years ago, one black American long resident in Thailand sent me a letter in which he commented on the effects of this relentless barrage of black athletic images. Based on what their media showed them, he reported, South Asians had no reason to believe that African-American abilities extended beyond the world of sports.

While it is tempting to reply that Americans know better than that, given our knowledge of what black people have done in many fields of endeavor, our own domestic reality still resembles the global stage that presents NBA stars and other pop culture icons as representative African Americans. That is why relieving black men of the involuntary athletic identity that has been inflicted on them over the past one hundred years is part of the unfinished business that faces American society in the twenty-first century. . . .

The essayist Gerald Early, for example, sees the black

fighter as a symbol of "what it means to be a black American." "One could argue," he adds, "that the three most important black figures in twentieth-century American culture were prizefighters: Jack Johnson, Joe Louis, and Muhammad Ali." This view finds support in a once-influential work of social science such as *The Mark of Oppression: Explorations in the Personality of the American Negro*. As the psychoanalysts Abram Kardiner and Lionel Ovesey listened to their black patients, they could observe the special role athletic heroes played in the minds of people whose lives had been deformed by a racial caste system. "Until recently," they wrote, "the Negro has had no real culture heroes with whom he could identify." They also concluded that athletes did not stimulate in black people the feelings of hostility and envy that could be directed at other black high achievers who had distinguished themselves in an academic setting. Whereas Joe Louis, Lena Home, and Jackie Robinson could be "accepted by most Negroes as common ideal figures," the "educated Negro technician" occupied a tenuous position located somewhere between his fellow blacks and the dominant whites.

This oppositional relationship between black athletic and academic achievement has persisted during the age of "black dominance" in the sports world that began in the 1960s. One difference between the age of segregation and the post–Civil Rights era is that, during the later period, dreams of athletic stardom have induced many black children to reject educational opportunities that simply did not exist for those who grew up idolizing Jackie Robinson during the 1940s and 1950s.

Today, over-identification with athletes and the world of physical performances limits the development of black children by discouraging academic achievement in favor of physical self-expression, which many blacks as well as whites consider a racial trait. Some educators understand that the self-absorbed style promoted by glamorous black athletes subverts intellectual development. For that reason, a school for black boys in Chicago several years ago adopted a policy of stylistic abstinence: "No gum-chewing is allowed. No sagging pants. No sunglasses, biker pants or tank tops. No earrings worn by boys. No designs carved in the hair"—in short, a complete repudiation of the showy male style flaunted by many black stars. Such policies aim at mitigating an intense peer pressure that equates academic excellence with effeminacy and racial disloyalty and identifies "blackness" with physical prowess. . . .

In *The Content of Our Character*, Shelby Steele's bestselling treatise on the emotional complexities of the African-American psyche, the author sees the focus on athletic achievement as a self-defeating defensive strategy, a way of staving off self-doubts that are continually being generated by academic failure. "Across the country thousands of young black males take every opportunity and make every effort to reach the elite ranks of the NBA or NFL," Steele writes. "But in the classroom, where racial vulnerability is a hidden terror, they and many of their classmates put forth the meagerest effort and show a virtual indifference to the genuine opportunity that is education.". . .

Nor is this behavior specifically African-American, since it is observed in other countries as well as in the United States. R. Patrick Solomon's *Black Resistance in High School* describes what he saw in a Canadian setting: "Embracing the school curriculum and such attendant activities as speaking standard English, spending a lot of time in the library, working hard to get good grades, and being on time were perceived as 'acting white.' Here again, black students who engaged in academic pursuits were labeled 'brainiacs' and were alienated, ostracized, or even physically assaulted by militant blacks." In a similar vein, Dr. Mamphela Ramphele, once a leading South African anti-apartheid activist and now vice chancellor of the University of Capetown, offered the following observation in 1997: "I find it interesting that we [blacks] are comfortable with sporting victories. We have only the best people representing us when it comes to those things. But not to when it comes to matters intellectual." But how could it be otherwise, given that an emphasis on the physicality of black people remains one of the enduring legacies of European colonialism?

The neocolonial logic of "black dominance" in the service of white-owned enterprises has been noted by a number of African-American observers. The idea that African Americans are over-invested in sport was first promoted during the modern period by the black sports activist and sociologist Harry Edwards a quarter-century ago. "Far from being a positive force in the development of the black masses," he wrote in 1973, "integrated big-time sport in its present form is perhaps a negative influence." "Sports provide the black fan with the illusion of spiritual reinforcement in his own life struggles." "Athletics, then, stifles the pursuit of rational alternatives by black people." Fifteen years later Edwards continued to make the case against this social trap: "Black families are four times more likely than White families to push their children toward sports-career aspirations—often to the neglect and detriment of other critically important areas of personal and cultural development." In 1992 Edwards was still writing of "an exaggerated and inordinate [Black] social and cultural emphasis upon sports achievement as a social and economic mobility vehicle." More recently, he has described the social circumstances of many young black men as so desperate that "exploiting black youths' overemphasis on sports participation and achievement may be our only remaining avenue" for educating and integrating them into American society.

In 1993 a black senior admissions officer at Harvard addressed the same topic:

> Unfortunately, TV images of black males are not particularly diverse. Their usual roles are to display physical prowess, sing, dance, play a musical instrument or make an audience laugh. These roles are enticing and generously rewarded. But the reality is that success comes to only a few extraordinarily gifted performers or athletes. . . . Millions see these televised roles as a definition of black men.

> Nowhere is this more misleading than in the inner city, where young males see it as the way out. . . . This powerful medium [television] has made the glamour of millionaire boxers, ballplayers, musicians and comedians appear so close, so tangible that, to naive young boys, it seems only a dribble or a dance step away. In the hot glare of such surrealism, schoolwork and prudent personal behavior can become irrelevant. . . .

In 1997 Northeastern University's Center for the Study of Sport in Society reported that 66% of African-American boys between the ages of 13 and 18 believed that they were capable of supporting themselves as professional athletes.

The prominent black psychiatrist and social activist Alvin Poussaint, a professor at Harvard Medical School, commented as follows: "There is an overemphasis on sports in the black community, and too many black students are putting all their eggs in one basket.". . .

Boys' Interest in Sports by Race

In 1997 *Sports Illustrated* conducted a poll of middle and high school students on sports and race. Below are some of the results regarding black children's career aspirations.

Kids' interest in playing team sports

	Black Males	White Males
Very Interested	77%	61%
Somewhat Interested	16%	23%
Not Too Interested	2%	10%
Not at All Interested	1%	5%

Percentage of kids who think they may be good enough to play a professional sport someday

	Black Males	White Males
Basketball	55%	20%
Football	49%	27%

Responses to the question, "Realistically, what could you become when you grow up?"

	Black Males	White Males
Pro Athlete	57%	41%
Lawyer	17%	27%
Teacher	14%	28%

Sports Illustrated, December 8, 1997.

The formation of social consciousness in Western societies has long included a racial typology that posits blacks and whites as polar opposites who differ both biologically and culturally. Only half a century ago discussion of such differences, both real and imagined, was accepted and quite uninhibited. As African Americans gained greater status and respect after the Second World War, the crudest and most ignorant assertions and speculations about racial differences were either discredited by more accurate information or entered into a state of suspended animation in which they could not be challenged by better informed ideas about race.

There is still a lot of such racial material floating around in people's heads, passed on from one generation to the next, because Western societies have done little to remove it. When, for example, the golfer Jack Nicklaus told an interviewer in 1994 that blacks were anatomically unsuited to play golf because they "have different muscles that react in different ways," he was invoking an eccentric racial biology of whose origins he was certainly unaware. In fact, the certainty with which he offered this fantasy was directly proportional to his indifference to where it had come from. It was simply and intuitively a fact about race. In a similar vein, I have heard people with no scientific training repeat mistaken dogmas about the bones and tendons of the "black" foot that supposedly give African-American sprinters their extra speed. These ideas appeared, and were discredited, during the 1930s. Yet there they were, like ancient dragonflies preserved in amber, floating out of brains that had somehow preserved them until the end of the twentieth century.

Racially integrated sport has preserved such racial folklore by giving the racial anthropology of the nineteenth century a new lease on life. The domination of various athletic events by specific ethnic or racial groups has promoted ideas about racial athletic aptitude throughout the twentieth century. Once upon a time the long-distance races were a specialty of the "stoic" Finns. Today it is darker-skinned stoics from North and East Africa. Nor is the racial folklore of sport a monopoly of the whites who have lost so much ground to fitter and darker competitors over the past generation. Black people absorb racial folklore with an efficiency that equals or exceeds that of whites, given their special emotional investment in athletic achievement and their awareness of the physical traumas endured by their ancestors. The notion that African Americans are the robust issue of breeding experiments has thus served the fantasy needs of blacks and whites alike. "We were simply bred for physical qualities," the Olympic champion sprinter Lee Evans said in 1971. Many other black athletes, as well as better-educated black men, have embraced the same eugenic myth. "Slavery," a black physician told the African-American medical association in 1962, "was the greatest biological experiment of all times. Slavery began with the trip to America, during which all of the weak ones were killed or thrown overboard or allowed to die. This was followed by the slave block, further selection and sales as desirable animals. From this point on, artificial mating occurred."

My research confirms what Franz Fanon pointed out in *Black Skin, White Masks* half a century ago, namely, that blacks and whites continue to ingest substantial quantities of a racial folklore that physicalizes black human beings while devaluing their minds. This demonstrates in turn the persisting influence of the nineteenth-century "law of compensation," which postulates an inverse relationship between brain and brawn. (The ubiquitous "dumb jock" stereotype is yet another version of this folk belief.) A long tradition of racist humor about black appetites for sex and food, the widespread popular belief in the eugenic breeding of slaves, the longevity of ideas about black immunities to pain and disease, the panracial belief in black athletic superiority—all of this confirms that black people have been identified with their bodies to an extraordinary degree.

The influence of such ideas on African Americans has never been studied in a systematic way. What we do know is that stereotypes of black athletic superiority are now firmly established as the most recent version of a racial folklore that has spread across the face of the earth over the past two centuries, and a corresponding belief in white athletic inferiority pervades popular thinking about racial difference. Such ideas probably do more than anything else in our public life to encourage the idea that blacks and whites are biologically different in meaningful ways. Conservative racial thinkers like Charles Murray and Dinesh D'Souza have declared that black athletic superiority is evidence of more profound racial differences, and there is no telling how many people, black and white, may agree with them.

The potential consequences of regarding oneself as essentially or uniquely physical by nature would thus include particular doubts about one's intelligence, the value of getting an education, and the idea of learning for its own sake. This relates in turn to the growing interest in why the academic performance of socially advantaged black children continues to lag behind that of white children of comparable social status. "How do we explain the underproductivity of middle-class kids, of able and gifted minority youngsters who come out of situations where you would expect high achievement?" asks Edmund W. Gordon, a professor emeritus of psychology at Yale University and the co-chairman of the National Task Force on Minority High Achievement. "This is not something that a lot of people feel comfortable talking about."

Explaining this phenomenon will require cultural anthropological analysis of a very high order. I would also suggest that productive thinking about this problem need not be monopolized by the experts. Any parent who takes the time to reflect on the intellectual formation of his or her children will be able to identify some of the factors that are likely to promote the development of intellectual interests and self-confidence. Such factors do not include a sense that one's primary aptitude is physical self-expression. That is why one of our goals should be the abolition of a social universe in which African-American schoolchildren cannot believe that the black college students who come to mentor them are not athletes, since television has persuaded them that every black person is an athlete.

*"African American student-athletes
understand that playing sports can help
them attain the educational, social, and life
skills that will benefit them as productive
members of society."*

A Preoccupation with Sports Is Not Detrimental to Black Youth

Richard E. Lapchick

Richard E. Lapchick is the founder and director of Northeastern University's Center for the Study of Sport in Society and the author of *Smashing Barriers: Race and Sport in the New Millennium*, from which the following article is excerpted. In it he maintains that participation in sports benefits all children and teenagers, especially African Americans and young women. Lapchick admits that many black children's hopes of becoming professional athletes are unrealistic, but he also cites survey results indicating that black student-athletes understand the importance of balancing athletics and academics. Moreover, he argues that sports help prepare all children to become responsible adults and help them stay out of trouble during their teenage years, particularly in urban areas.

As you read, consider the following questions:

1. What Boston program does Lapchick point to as a model for encouraging youth participation in sports?
2. What percentage of African American student athletes surveyed said that sports helped them avoid drugs and alcohol, respectively?

Richard E. Lapchick, *Smashing Barriers: Race and Sport in the New Millennium*. Lanham, MD: Madison Books, 2001. Copyright © 1991 by Richard E. Lapchick. Updated edition copyright © 2001 by Richard E. Lapchick. All rights reserved. Reproduced by permission.

I wrote this [viewpoint] during the 2000 presidential campaign in which politicians once again called for a "balanced budget." Funding for education was targeted as a budget buster. At the high school level, sports programs frequently seemed to be the first to be cut.

While students' test scores decline, drugs, gangs, and violence thrive in many secondary and even elementary schools. There is no doubt that we need new sources of revenue to pull our nation out of the educational crisis we are in today. Problems are especially acute in urban areas, although events such as the school violence in Springfield, Oregon; Pearl, Mississippi; and Jonesboro, Arkansas, remind us that it is not just urban America that is suffering. Part of the answer is increased funding for education. Calls for increased allotments for mathematics, the sciences, and language arts have a compelling and clear purpose. The necessity of attracting and keeping good teachers with better economic incentives is just as indisputable.

In this context, sport is often viewed as an expensive frill, as the "toy department." However, because participating in sports can be a strong source of self-esteem, cutting or eliminating school sports programs may strike one more blow at the likelihood of kids from lower socioeconomic backgrounds breaking the cycle of historic discrimination that traps so many.

All data shows that school-age children are more likely to get into trouble between the hours of three and six P.M. If we take away the sports activities that occupy nearly twenty percent of our students during those hours, we markedly enlarge the opportunities for trouble. Many families are now headed by two working parents or by a single working parent who is not at home at 3 P.M. when students return from school. Too often a child at home alone turns to trash television. If they have escaped witnessing violence first hand, it becomes part of their viewing patterns, a normal and acceptable part of life.

There is too little for kids to do in the afternoon or on weekends in our cities. Budget cuts have already closed many recreation centers, zoos, playgrounds, and ballparks that kids used to flock to after school. The supervision provided in organized sport provides structure to children participating. It is time for corporate America to invest in youth sport as another way to provide children with a safety net. The lure of joining gangs can be offset by the benefits of joining teams. Donna Lopiano poignantly spelled it out in a 1999 article for *The Sports Business Journal:* "Kids join gangs because they want respect (applause), support (coaches who care), family (teammates), recognition (batting titles, golden glove awards, or simply a salute from another player), an identity (athlete), control (responsibility for their own performance), and the future promise of money. They want structure (the "game," the team, and the rules). Most of all they want belonging."

Sports Outreach Programs

In 1998, Boston began Urban Youth Sports (UYS), a major grassroots effort to increase access to youth sports through a partnership between the City of Boston, Northeastern University's Center for the Study of Sport in Society, and several corporate partners including Reebok, Blue Cross/Blue Shield, Partners Health, the Harvard School of Public Health, and the Robert Wood Johnson Foundation.

The Boston Youth Sports Needs Assessment Survey, sponsored by UYS, documented the compelling needs of young people in Boston, which experts say has a typical youth sport profile. Some of their findings follow:

- Just over one third of school-age children in the City of Boston participate in organized youth sports, compared to nearly 90 percent in the suburbs.
- Only 40 percent of boys and less than 15 percent of girls play sports.
- Suburban girls have six times more opportunities to play sports than city girls do.
- City parents are only half as likely as suburban parents to attend games, due to poor public transportation and other factors.
- Most funding in the city goes to one or two sports, usually basketball or baseball, at the elite youth levels.

At the same time, many adults are increasingly wary of sports. Extraordinary salaries, unethical administrators, and unruly athletes have taken away the luster of sporting events. Suggestions to cut high school sports programs or close another recreation center do not meet the resistance they once did.

Yet according to innumerable studies and surveys, the value of sport to its youthful participants is incontrovertible. When asked, boys and girls list "fun" as the most important reason they play. But for African Americans and women, there are much more compelling reasons.

According to a national survey of 865 high-school students conducted by Lou Harris, many African American student-athletes still harbor unrealistic aspirations to stardom. Fifty-one percent of African American high-school athletes believed they would make the pros (vs. 18 percent of white student-athletes).

Fourteen-year-old African Americans, recognize that the color of their skin will, in all likelihood, limit the range of their life choices. Statistically they are less likely to finish high school, to go to college, and to be employed than if they were white. They have far fewer chances of making it big in corporate America as a top administrator or of being hired as a college professor. Just turn on a television and you will not see many African Americans in such professions.

But turn on a Los Angeles Lakers game and you will see Kobe Bryant making more money per quarter than the average high school teacher does per year. The 51 percent who think they will make it are, in their terms, making a somewhat logical choice. Don't tell them that they can't beat the 10,000 to one odds.

In communities driven by despair, athletes in outreach programs realized that they could not afford to snuff out hope. So, while not throwing sand on the fires of desire, athletes have been telling young people to keep hope alive and balance it with preparation for a future that does not include a career as a professional athlete.

Balancing Sports and Academics

The Harris survey indicated that professional athletes in outreach programs have had a substantial and a sustained impact and that African American student-athletes understand that playing sports can help them attain the educational, social, and life skills that will benefit them as productive members of society. They don't have to play for the Lakers. They can be the team doctor or attorney. This study gives us hope that fantasies of a career in professional sports may not lead to shock and emotional letdown. The study highlighted three important issues that follow:

- Seventy-six percent of African American and 60 percent of white student-athletes favored a minimum "C" average for eligibility in sports, demonstrating their understanding of the need to balance athletics and academics. The student-athletes were *asking* for a higher standard. As of 1990, more than forty states did not require a "C" average to participate in high school sports. We are failing them by not asking for more.
- As drop-out rates in urban communities soared, 57 percent of African American student-athletes felt that playing sports encouraged them "a great deal" to stay in school.
- Fifty percent of African American student-athletes believed that playing sports helped them "a great deal" to become a better student.

Apparently, most student-athletes don't ignore academic preparation even if they believe they will make the pros. The Harris survey was the first conclusive evidence that concerned athletes and school administrators have finally reached these young people after a decade of messages begging them to balance academic and athletic goals.

Playing sports has even more clear social benefits for African American students. While drugs and alcohol dominate the lives of many teenagers, sport seemed to help African American student-athletes avoid such potential dangers. Sixty-five percent of African American student-athletes responded that playing sports had helped them "a great deal" to avoid drugs while 60 percent believed that playing sports had the same effect on their ability to abstain from alcohol use.

While society as a whole seems to grow increasingly fearful of urban youth, 44 percent of all African American student-athletes believed that playing sports had helped them "a great deal" to become better citizens. Lou Harris noted that "it was critical to see that at a time when racial and ethnic tensions boil over in school into serious conflicts almost every day, the survey showed that team sports create friendships that cut across racial lines." Seventy-six percent of all white and African American student-athletes reported that they became friends with someone from another racial or ethnic group through playing sports.

Encouraging African American Children to "Go for It"

I am always puzzled by Black people who, in an earnest attempt to encourage Black youngsters to consider careers in fields other than sports, resort to comments such as, "We don't need any more Black athletes."

Of course, it is true that only a few of those who pursue careers in professional sports wind up realizing their dreams. And there is a need for students to consider the vast number of opportunities in other professions. But does that mean we should be discouraging Black students from pursuing opportunities and careers in sports?

I think not. . . .

The problem isn't that there are too many Black athletes. It is that we've not been able to replicate our success on the playing field in other career endeavors.

Heck, we've only recently begun to replicate the critical mass we have on the field in the sporting industry's executive offices. But one reason we now have access to these executive jobs is because successful athletes like Arthur Ashe, Kareem Abdul Jabbar, Michael Jordan and Jackie Joyner-Kersee helped to create those opportunities.

Rather than steering our kids away from sports, we should capitalize on our past success by encouraging as many who demonstrate the interest or the talent to go for it.

Cheryl D. Fields, "Point: Sports Can Build Up Black Women in Society," *Black Issues in Higher Education*, April 27, 2000.

Americans of different races are not together as equals in many places. In our racially charged society, this may prove to be the ultimate benefit of sport, finally fulfilling part of the dream of Jackie Robinson.

The Benefits of Sports for Young Women

What about the impact of sport on young women's lives?
- In 1998, the Women's Sports Foundation Report: Sport and Teen Pregnancy shows how playing sports reduced

a teenage girl's chances of becoming pregnant.

- By participating in sport for four hours a week, a girl can reduce her chance of developing breast cancer by up to 60 percent.
- Girls who play sports have better grades and are more likely to graduate.
- Girls who play sports are more self-confident, have stronger self-images, and higher self-esteem.
- Eighty percent of female executives in Fortune 500 companies played sports as children.

How important is youth sport to girls? If a girl is not involved in sport by the age of ten, she has less than a 10 percent chance of playing a sport at age twenty-five, thus increasing the chances of a less healthy lifestyle with greater health risks. Girls and boys who play sports together as youths are more likely to work well together through childhood, and adolescence and into adulthood. As adults, they may be more inclined to become mentors, coaches, and corporate sponsors who give back to their community because their personal stake in giving back was increased by youth league and high school athletic participation. Children's chances for healthy development are markedly increased when they play sport.

Provide More Resources for Youth Sports Programs

Sport is not a panacea. But without it, more obstacles get in the way of the people in our nation who have had the smallest chances of reaching the top rungs in the worlds of business, academics, and, yes, even sports. In addition to other preventative programs, the nation must train coaches and establish organized athletic opportunities for urban youth, especially girls, as an integral part of promoting healthy living for young people.

Investments of money and people-power can help remove most of the obstacles to meaningful participation, but it will take the will of government and partnerships between business, the academic community, and youth sport leaders. Boston, Detroit, and the California bay area are setting the example for programs every city in the nation should imitate.

Boston has assumed leadership in the effort to support and coordinate sports programs for urban children regardless of race, gender, ethnicity, and class or family structure. In 1998, Boston's Mayor Thomas Menino emphasized his determination to raise future fiscal support for urban youth sport. "I'd like to see every kid in the City of Boston participating," Menino said. "We'll find the money for this. We always do."

As the presidential debates continued with more and more talk of a balanced budget, I argued that America needed more, not fewer, resources for education. Every city in America needs high school sports programs, open recreation centers, and more urban youth sports leagues. Sports participation can help keep today's youth from becoming tomorrow's subjects of crime stories in the news. It can help give *all* children the chance to participate in the presidential debates of the twenty-first century when it becomes their time to lead America.

> *"The least [professional athletes] could do is set a better example. Not because of the money, because so many look up to them."*

Professional Athletes Should Be Better Role Models

Mark Patinkin

In the following viewpoint Mark Patinkin argues that too many professional athletes engage in unsportsmanlike behavior on the field and in criminal behavior in their private lives. He contrasts the poor examples that professional athletes set with the class and courtesy of the youth players in the 2003 Little League World Series. Because so many children look up to them, he concludes, athletes should try to be better role models. Patinkin is a writer for the *Providence Journal*.

As you read, consider the following questions:

1. What two examples of sportsmanship in the 2003 Little League World Series does the author say are unprecedented in the major leagues?
2. What unsportsmanlike behavior does Patinkin say children started mimicking after seeing baseball pro Roberto Alomar do it?
3. According to the author, how much does a great seat to a Red Sox game now cost?

Mark Patinkin, "The Kids Know What the Game Is All About," *Providence Journal*, August 26, 2003, p. G01. Copyright © 2003 by Knight-Ridder/Tribune News Service. Reproduced by permission.

So I'm watching a baseball game on ESPN, and thinking a thought I seldom have about sports stars anymore. I'm thinking that these players truly are role models. And that with luck, certain others can learn good behavior from them.

Which others?

Oh, professional athletes. See, the ESPN game was part of the Little League World Series.

I'd like to tell you about a couple of stunning moments.

The first happened during the consolation battle for third place between the Saugus, Massachusetts, team and the Caribbean team. The Caribbean pitcher, a big 12-year-old named Tharick Martines, threw a 70 mile-per-hour fastball that hit a Saugus batter named Michael Scuzzarella in the chest. Play stopped for five minutes while the trainers checked him, finally, he stood and trotted to first at which point, Martines loped over, apologized to Scuzzarella and shook his hand. The gesture surprised the announcers, one of who finally said, "That's what the game is all about."

If I've ever seen a moment with that much class on a major league ballfield, I can't remember it.

Usually, it's the opposite. Like when New York Mets catcher Mike Piazza swung and broke his bat during the World Series a few years ago, and Yankees pitcher Roger Clemens picked up a piece of the wood and flung it back at Piazza. There was no good explanation for it, except that pro athletes seem more primed for bluster and menace than sportsmanship.

On Saturday [August 23], the Saugus team played Boynton Beach, Florida, for the U.S. title. Boynton Beach won.

The Florida team rushed to embrace each other, but then did something that has almost no precedent among the pros. They invited the Saugus kids to join their victory lap. Together, the two teams jogged around the field, sharing the applause.

They sure didn't learn such graciousness from the pros.

Professional Athletes Set Poor Examples

Think of the time Roberto Alomar spit on an umpire because he disagreed with a call. Later, Bob Still of the National Association of Sports Officials said his group had never heard of a youth player doing that—until after Alomar did it. At which point youth umpires reported a number of spitting incidents by kids. Nice example, Roberto.

Think of the fact that NBA and NFL players are so routinely arrested for assault, domestic abuse and drugs that newspaper sports sections often run a wrap-up under the heading "In the courts"—which is not a reference to any playing surface.

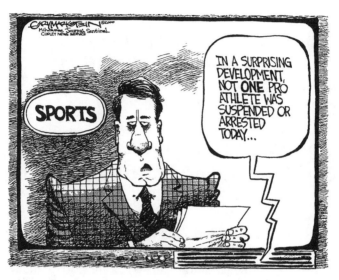

Markstein. © 2000 by Copley News Service. Reproduced by permission.

Think about how pro athletes hold out for $13 million a year because $11 million isn't enough. The result? If you want to get a great seat to a big Red Sox game now, ticket agencies will be charging $450 or more.

A few years ago, I saw the Chicago Bulls play at their home stadium, in an inner city neighborhood where kids dream under netless playground rims. Except the stadium was filled with well-off suburbanites, in part because superstars, and even medium stars, demand millions per year.

The least these guys could do is set a better example. Not because of the money, because so many look up to them.

But few do.

"That's what the game is all about," the announcer said of the Little Leaguers.

The pros could learn from them.

> "*Everyone must remember that athletes are paid to play a game. They are not saving lives, and they are not making the world a better place on a daily basis.*"

Professional Athletes Should Not Be Viewed as Role Models

Ashley Brown

Ashley Brown argues in the following viewpoint that athletes should not be viewed as role models. In Brown's view, this is not because some athletes engage in unsportsmanlike or criminal behavior—most athletes, she writes, try to conduct themselves in a decent manner. Rather, Brown maintains that professional athletes are getting paid to play a game and are not as praiseworthy as people who have chosen professions which truly help others, such as teaching, firefighting, and nursing. Brown was a journalism student at Ohio State University at the time that she wrote this viewpoint.

As you read, consider the following questions:
1. What famous athletes who are often considered role models does the author name?
2. In the author's opinion, how does the Kobe Bryant case demonstrate the inappropriateness of viewing professional athletes as role models?
3. In Brown's view, what criteria should an individual meet in order to be considered a role model?

Ashley Brown, "Are Players Role Models?" *The Lantern*, December 5, 2003. Reproduced by permission.

The term "role model" is thrown around quite a bit in the world of professional sports.

Many athletes such as Eddie George, Peyton Manning and Derek Jeter have been deemed role models because of their stellar athletic ability and impressive on-camera conduct. But the public will never truly know how most athletes behave off-camera and it is for this reason that athletes cannot be role models.

Although the media reports both the public and private lives of professional athletes, what we learn about those athletes is, for the most part, what they want us to learn. With some obvious exceptions—Dennis Rodman and Mike Tyson—most players attempt to portray themselves in a positive light when in public.

But looks can be deceiving, as Kobe Bryant has so aptly demonstrated. I know, I know, I am tired of hearing about him too, but he provides a perfect example.

From Day One in the NBA, Bryant was given more press coverage than most pro athletes and was perceived to be a "good guy" because of his aptitude on the court and his quiet, polite demeanor off it.

Then Bryant was arrested and taken to court for alleged sexual assault. No one but he and the accuser know whether or not he is guilty, but everyone now knows that he is a cheater. The infamous purple diamond Bryant purchased for his wife shows that he is not above trying to buy forgiveness.

No matter the court verdict, Bryant already has proven that he is not of the high moral character many had once believed he was. He shows us that, no matter how much time the media may devote to a player, the public can never truly know him.

Merely Doing Their Jobs

Another factor preventing athletes from becoming role models is the fact that they play a game for a living. I realize that pro athletes work incredibly hard for their success, and I am not denying them their due credit for that dedication.

Every season, they spend hours in the weight room and on the practice field. They continually break down tape and, no matter how good an athlete may be, he is always trying to improve his level of play.

Many spend days, even weeks, away from their families. Their job permeates every aspect of their lives, making it less of a job and more of a lifestyle.

I know that many of them do wonderful things for their communities. They give time and money to charities, visit sick children in the hospital or coach sports camps for area children. But hard work and philanthropy alone do not make someone a role model.

Athletes and Social Activism

If I'm [professional golfer] Tiger Woods, I stick to what I do best. I hit the ball very hard and very far, I never three putt, I make the occasional commercial, I go home and watch the *Sopranos*. That's my life, no need to change it. Just because some nameless politician is out there championing a cause, doesn't mean that my star power is needed to give it a fighting chance. That's what politicians do, they affect social change through the government. It may be slow, it may be tedious, but that is their job. I hit a small ball into a small hole, end of story. . . .

Tiger Woods is an athlete, not a role model. He's not your anesthesiologist, he's not your psychologist, he's not really any kind of -ist. Assigning undue responsibilities to a star that the American public has created is not the way to affect social change.

David Shaw, "I Am Not a Role Model," www.sportsunabridged.com/su/080902.htm.

Everyone must remember that athletes are paid to play a game. They are not saving lives, and they are not making the world a better place on a daily basis. It could be argued that they are making the world better by providing entertainment for millions of people, but life would go on without sports. It would be different, but it would continue.

Others Deserve More Admiration

Life would be dramatically different if not for doctors, nurses, firemen, policemen, teachers and members of the military. I realize there are corrupt individuals in every profession, but, for the most part, those who have chosen to make their life's work helping others, are special and deserve the respect and admiration of others much more so than someone who plays a game for a living.

I do not dislike sports or the athletes who play them. In fact, sports have been a guiding force throughout my life, and I have spent countless hours playing and watching them. I am also not implying that all athletes are bad people—many deserve respect.

The bottom line is that athletes should not be role models. They can be admired for their hard work and dedication, but role models should come from within an individual's inner circle of family and friends.

Periodical Bibliography

The following articles have been selected to supplement the diverse views presented in this chapter.

American Demographics	"Good Sports," October 1, 2002.
Vernon L. Andrews	"Black Field of Dreams," *Society*, March 2000.
David Batstone	"Why Kids Hate Sports," *Sojourners*, July 2001.
Lisa Belkin	"A Silent Drain on Time: Children's Sports," *New York Times*, April 28, 2002.
Glen Cook	"Win at All Costs," *American School Board Journal*, August 2003.
CQ Researcher	"Is Bad Behavior Ruining American Sports?" March 23, 2001.
Cheryl D. Fields	"Point: Sports Can Build Up Black Women in Society," *Black Issues in Higher Education*, April 27, 2000.
P. David Halstead	"Seeking to Make Youth Sports Safe," *USA Today Magazine*, July 2001.
Mary Lord	"Dangerous Games," *U.S. News & World Report*, April 8, 2002.
Bob Morris	"Fielding Life's Grounders," *New York Times*, April 21, 2002.
S.L. Price	"Too Single-Minded?: Many Young Blacks Are So Intent on Becoming the Next Jordan That They Forego More Realistic Paths to Success," *Sports Illustrated*, December 8, 1997.
Michael L. Sachs	"Lighten Up, Parents!" *USA Today Magazine*, November 2000.
Sports Illustrated	"Out of Control," July 24, 2000.
Alexander Wolff	"The American Athlete, Age 10," *Sports Illustrated*, October 6, 2003.
Woman's Day	"Fans or Fanatics?" November 1, 2003.

CHAPTER 2

Should College Sports Be Reformed?

Chapter Preface

The issue of college sports reform is a perennial one in the sports world. At the heart of the matter is the fact that the nation's best men's college basketball and football teams have become almost as popular—and profitable—as their professional counterparts. For these colleges—mainly the schools in the National Collegiate Athletic Association (NCAA)—fielding a basketball or football teams is as much about television and advertising revenues as it is about athletics and school pride. And for many of the athletes on these teams, going to college is as much about auditioning for a job in the NBA or NFL as it is about getting an education.

The close relationship between big-time college athletics and professional sports is demonstrated by the case of Maurice Clarett, who led the Ohio State University Buckeyes in rushing in his 2002 freshman year. In 2003 Clarett initiated a legal challenge to the NFL rule that limits draft eligibility to players who have been out of high school for at least three years.

The NFL maintains that its policy ensures that players are "physically and emotionally" ready to enter the professional ranks. Clarett and his lawyer argued that the rule constitutes age discrimination. A federal judge sided with Clarett in February 2004, but a higher court issued a stay on the lower court's ruling, keeping the NFL rule in force and excluding Clarett from the 2004 draft.

The legal aspects of the case center on NFL policies, but they also raise the broader issue of how the NFL benefits from college football. "The pros have what amounts to a free minor-league system paid for by the colleges," writes *Akron Beacon Journal* columnist Terry Pluto, "and the colleges benefit by having instant stars like Clarett around for at least three years to win games, draw fans and make money for the school."

The Clarett case is one of many that raises questions about whether college athletes are treated unfairly. The authors in the following chapter examine this and other issues facing big-time college sports.

"The time has come to end the pretense that players in big-time college sports are amateurs."

College Athletes Should Be Paid

D. Stanley Eitzen

D. Stanley Eitzen is professor emeritus of sociology at Colorado State University, former president of the North American Society for the Sociology of Sport, and the author of *Fair and Foul: Beyond the Myths and Paradoxes of Sport.* In the following viewpoint he argues that athletes who play in big-time college sports programs are treated unfairly. The colleges and universities with the most successful and popular men's football and basketball teams, he contends, receive millions of dollars in television and advertising revenues, as does the National Collegiate Athletic Association, the governing body of big-time college sports. Many coaches are also paid over $1 million a year. Meanwhile, the athletes who comprise these million-dollar teams are forbidden to receive money, gifts, or other remuneration for their performance. The author concludes that college athletes should be paid, in proportion to the revenues their teams generate.

As you read, consider the following questions:

1. How many college football coaches were paid more than $1 million in 2000, according to Eitzen?
2. How much profit did Georgetown University make as a result of Patrick Ewing's four years of basketball play at the school in the early 1980s, in Eitzen's view?

D. Stanley Eitzen, "Slaves of Big-Time College Sports," *USA Today Magazine*, vol. 129, September 2000, p. 26. Copyright © 2000 by the Society for the Advancement of Education. Reproduced by permission.

The governing body of big-time college sports, the NCAA [National Collegiate Athletic Association], is caught in a huge contradiction—trying to reconcile a multibillion-dollar industry while claiming it is really an amateur activity. That it is a huge moneymaking industry is beyond dispute.

- The major conferences have an eight-year package (ending in 2006) worth $930,000,000 with ABC to televise the Bowl Championship Series (BCS) at the conclusion of the regular football season. Each team playing in a BCS game currently receives about $13,000,000 and, under the terms of the new contract, will receive around $17,000,000 in the final years of the agreement. Since the teams share these monies with their conference members, the 62 schools involved will divide approximately $116,000,000 in payouts annually.
- The NCAA has signed a $6,200,000,000, 11-year deal giving CBS the rights to televise its men's basketball championship. (That's $545,000,000 a year, up from the $216,000,000 annually with the current arrangement that expires after the 2002 tournament.) The NCAA also makes money from advertising and gate receipts for this tournament. To enhance gate receipts, the finals are always scheduled in huge arenas with seating capacities of at least 30,000, rather than normal basketball-sized venues.
- Universities sell sponsorships to various enterprises for advertising. The athletic department of the University of Colorado, for example, has 50 corporate sponsors. The major one is Coors Brewing Co., which has a $300,000 advertising package for scoreboard, radio, and TV advertising, plus a sign on the mascot's trailer. The school also named its basketball arena the Coors Event Center in return for a $5,000,000 donation.
- Nine football coaches will be paid at least $1,000,000 in overall compensation in 2000. . . .

Obviously, big-time athletic programs are commercial enterprises. The irony is that, while sports events generate millions for each school, the workers are not paid. Economist Andrew Zimbalist has written that "Big-time intercollegiate athletics is a unique industry. No other industry in the United States manages not to pay its principal producers a wage or a salary." The universities and the NCAA claim their athletes in big-time sports programs are amateurs and, despite the money generated, the NCAA and its member schools are amateur organizations promoting an educational mission. This amateur status is vitally important to the plantation owners in two regards. First, by not paying the athletes what they are worth, the schools' expenses are minimized, thus making the enterprises more profitable. Second, since athletic departments and the NCAA are considered part of the educational mission, they do not pay taxes on their millions from television, sponsorships, licensing, the sale of sky boxes and season tickets, and gate receipts. Moreover, contributions by individuals and corporations to athletic departments are tax-deductible.

The Injustice of Amateurism

To keep big-time college sports "amateur," the NCAA has devised a number of roles that eliminate all economic benefits to the athletes: They may receive only educational benefits (i.e., room, board, tuition, fees, and books); cannot sign with an agent and retain eligibility; cannot do commercials; cannot receive meals, clothing, transportation, or other gifts by individuals other than family members; and their relatives cannot receive gifts of travel to attend games or other forms of remuneration.

These rules reek with injustice. Athletes can make money for others, but not for themselves. Their coaches have agents, as may students engaged in other extracurricular activities, but the athletes cannot. Athletes are forbidden to engage in advertising, but their coaches are permitted to endorse products for generous compensation. Corporate advertisements are displayed in the arenas where they play, but with no payoff to the athletes. The shoes and equipment worn by the athletes bear very visible corporate logos, for which the schools are compensated handsomely. The athletes make public appearances for their schools and their photographs are used to publicize the athletic department and sell tickets, but they cannot benefit. The schools sell memorabilia and paraphernalia that incorporate the athletes' likenesses, yet only the schools pocket the royalties. The athletes cannot receive gifts, but coaches and other athletic department personnel receive the free use of automobiles, country club memberships, housing subsidies, etc.

Putting the Amateur Myth to Rest

Meaningful collegiate sports reform is impossible without first unmasking the NCAA's amateur myth. Once this myth has been dispelled, there are a number of options available to universities. One is for the majority of schools to give up athletic scholarships, return college sport to regular students, and get on with the task of educating America's youth. The other is to openly admit that scholarship athletes are paid professionals and to provide a nonexploitative context in which they can further develop their athletic skills. This second alternative would allow universities to operate a number of college sports teams primarily as profit centers and as training grounds for high performance athletes.

One fairly straightforward and workable approach to creating a nonexploitative model of professional college sport is to follow the contours of what exists now. The NCAA's Division IA would be set aside for schools that currently run one or more sports as unrelated businesses. What would be different is that sports in this category would have to be totally self-supporting. Money for administrative expenses, stadium upkeep, and other items that are often taken from the university's general fund would now come from sports revenues. Of course, line items such as coaches' salaries, player compensation, and travel and recruiting expenses would also be the total responsibility of each college sport franchise.

Allen L. Sack and Ellen J. Staurowsky, *College Athletes for Hire: The Evolution and Legacy of the NCAA's Amateur Myth.* Westport, CT: Praeger, 1998.

Most significantly, coaches receive huge deals from shoe companies (e.g., Duke University basketball coach Mike Krzyzewski has a 15-year shoe endorsement deal with Adidas, including a $1,000,000 bonus plus $375,000 annually), while the players are limited to wearing that corporation's shoes and apparel. An open market operates when it comes to revenue for coaches, resulting in huge pay packages for the top names, but not so for star players. When a coach is fired or resigns, he often receives a "golden parachute," which sometimes is in the multimillion-dollar category, while players who leave a program early receive nothing but vilification for being disloyal. When a team is invited to a bowl game, it means an extra month of practice for the athletes, while head coaches, depending on the bowl venue, receive generous bonuses. A university entourage of administrators and their spouses accompany the team to the bowl game with all expenses paid, while the parents and spouses of the athletes have to pay their own way.

As an extreme example, an analysis of the economic impact of basketball star Patrick Ewing to Georgetown University during his four years there in the early 1980s shows that he brought more than $12,000,000 to the school (a tripling of attendance, increased television revenues, and qualifying for the NCAA tournament each year). Meanwhile, the cost to Georgetown for Ewing's services totaled $48,600—providing a tidy profit of $11,951,400 for the university. A study by an economist almost a decade ago found that top-level college football players at that time generated a net gain (subtracting room, board, tuition, and books) of more than $2,000,000 over a four-year period.

What exactly are the wages of average college athletes in the major sports? The answer is a bit complicated since those who do not graduate have not taken advantage of their tuition, so they have played only for their room and board. Moreover, there is a significant difference in tuition costs between state and private universities. Economist Richard G. Sheehan has calculated the hourly wage of big-time college players taking these considerations into account and assuming a workload of 1,000 hours per year. The best pay received, he found, occurred at private schools with high graduation rates for the athletes; the lowest, at state schools with low graduation rates. Duke, for instance, paid an equivalent of $20.37 an hour for its football players, compared to the University of Texas–El Paso's $3.51. The median wage at all big-time schools was $6.82 an hour for basketball players and $7.69 an hour for football players. . . .

Dismal Graduation Rates

Since most college athletes never play at the professional level, the attainment of a college degree is a crucial determinant for their upward mobility, and thus a rationale for tolerating the unjust plantation system. Yet, graduation from college, while not the long shot of becoming a professional athlete, is also a bad bet.

A 1999 report compiled by the NCAA examined Division I athletes who enrolled in 1992–93 to determine how many had graduated after six years. (Athletes who left school in good academic standing were not counted in the results.) The data show that, while the overall graduation rate for all male students was 54%, for football players it was 50% (60% for whites and 42% for blacks) and 41% for male basketball players (53% for whites and 33% for blacks). While some programs are exemplary (Duke graduated 92% of its football players and Stanford University graduated 100% of its men's basketball players over the six-year period), others are not. According to *Emerge* magazine, 38 Division I basketball teams did not graduate a single black player in 1998. From 1995 to 1999, Ohio State graduated 100% of its female basketball players, but just 31% of its male basketball players. The 1999 men's basketball NCAA Division I champion, the University of Connecticut, managed to graduate a mere 29% of its team members between 1994 and 1997.

There are several reasons for the relatively low graduation rates for big-time college athletes. Compared to nonathletes, they are less prepared for college. On average, they enter in the bottom quarter of the freshman class (based on SAT scores). Football and men's basketball players in big-time sports programs are more than six times as likely as other students to receive special treatment in the admissions process—that is, they are admitted below the standard requirements for their universities. Second, athletes spend 30–40 hours a week on their sport, which is demanding, as well as physically and mentally fatiguing. Third, an anti-intellectual atmosphere is common within the jock subculture. Finally, some athletes attend college not for the education, but because they believe it will lead to a professional career. In this regard, former Iowa State University football coach Jim Walden has said, "Not more than 20% of the football players go to college for an education."

Not only do typical athletes in big-time sports enter at an academic disadvantage, they often encounter a diluted educational experience while attending their schools. Coaches, under the intense pressure to win, tend to diminish the student side of their athletes by counseling them to take easy courses, choose easy majors, and enroll in courses given by faculty members friendly to the athletic department. Some of the more unscrupulous have altered transcripts, given athletes answers to exams, staged phantom courses, and hired surrogate test takers. In one well-publicized case of academic fraud, a tutor for the University of Minnesota athletic department wrote more than 400 papers for basketball players over five years. Even with that help, just 23% of the players recruited since 1986 to play basketball at that university have graduated, the worst rate of any Big Ten basketball team during that period. . . .

Changing the System

The obvious starting point for changing the system is to pay athletes in the revenue-producing sports fair compensation for the revenues they generate. Athletes should receive a monthly stipend for living expenses, insurance coverage, and paid trips home during holidays and for family emergencies. Media basketball commentator Dick Vitale suggests a modest plan to make the system somewhat fairer. He says that the NCAA should invest $1,000,000,000 of the $6,200,000,000 it will receive to broadcast the NCAA men's basketball tournament and pay the athletes $250 a month. *Sports Illustrated* writer E.M. Swift responded: "Is Vitale right on the money? You make the call. For now, as the NCAA continues to treat its athletes with supercilious contempt while reaping GNP-sized windfalls from their labor, you can at least say this for scholarship athletes: They're getting a free education in no-holds-barred capitalism."

The time has come to end the pretense that players in big-time college sports are amateurs. They are paid through a scholarship, far from a just or living wage in this world of big-time sports megabucks.

"The notion that a full scholarship isn't a fair exchange for athletic services provided to a university . . . is ridiculous."

College Athletes Should Not Be Paid

Jason Whitlock

Jason Whitlock is a regular columnist for the *Kansas City Star* and the host of a sports radio talk show. In the following viewpoint he discusses the Chris Webber scandal, in which it was revealed that Webber, a star basketball player at the University of Michigan from 1992 to 1996, and some of his teammates received thousands of dollars from Ed Martin, a gambler and former Michigan booster. Martin was arrested on charges of money laundering, and the revelation led to still-unproven suspicions that Webber and his teammates might have engaged in point-shaving (purposefully keeping a game's score close for the benefit of gamblers) at Martin's request. Whitlock maintains that the incident debunks the myth that big-time college athletes do not receive adequate compensation for their play. He also argues that a scholarship is more than adequate compensation for a student's contributions to a school's sports program.

As you read, consider the following questions:
1. What claim did Webber make during his college years about how little money he had, as paraphrased by Whitlock?
2. How do many college athletes allow themselves to be exploited, in Whitlock's opinion?

Jason Whitlock, "College Athletes Already Paid in Full," www.espn.com, September 19, 2002. Copyright © 2002 by Jason Whitlock. Reproduced by permission.

I have no idea how much money Chris Webber and his Fab Five teammates received from old-school numbers man Ed Martin while they led the University of Michigan to back-to-back NCAA [National Collegiate Athletic Association] title games. In the two years I covered the Fab Five for the *Ann Arbor (Michigan) News*, I never met Ed Martin. Never even had a two-minute discussion about him.

I do know only a fool would watch Webber, Jalen Rose and Juwan Howard drive up to practice and games in new SUVs, gaudy jewelry dangling from their necks and expensive leather coats and jackets wrapped around their shoulders and not suspect the Fab Five had a nice source of income.

I do know only a man or woman devoid of his senses couldn't smell the sense of financial entitlement that wafted from the five teenagers as they made college basketball history and, in their minds, made middle-aged white businessmen wealthy.

The Injustice Myth

But somehow many of us missed it. We chose instead to believe the myths. When Webber laughably claimed that he was frustrated because he couldn't afford to buy a Big Mac at McDonald's while local vendors sold his jersey for $50, we lapped the story up and cried about the injustice of the NCAA not paying its athletes.

We're part of the problem. We, the media, can blame Webber and the Fab Five for sticking their hands out and accepting what was given to them, but that's pretty much what we told them to do. For the past 20 years, ever since college football and men's basketball have become big, big business, we've wrongly told college athletes they've been getting ripped off. The NCAA should give them something, at least money to go to the movies and do their laundry.

And the whole time we've been singing the sad song about athletes getting screwed financially, we've been hypocritically complaining about the so-called "street agents" who are lining the pockets of the athletes and allegedly undermining their morals.

This is so silly. By constantly beating the drum that college athletes are getting screwed, we created the market for "street agents" to flourish. And I say this in all seriousness, we've given "street agents" a bad name.

I suspect if Ed Martin is anything like my grandfather who ran "numbers" in an Indianapolis automotive plant in the 1960s and '70s, he's a respected man in his community. He's not some violent, game-fixing, Mafia gambling king-pin. "Numbers" men are prevalent in the black community. They were even more popular before our government moved into their industry with state-sponsored daily lotter-ies and Pick 3s.

I'm not throwing a pity party for Martin. He evaded pay-ing taxes on large sums of money. He deserves the jail time he's about to receive. It's just that we need to view him in proper context. I'm sure he loaned money to and did favors for more Detroiters than just the city's top athletes. We, the media, call Martin a "street agent." I bet the people who gambled with Martin on the job viewed him as a dear friend and saw him no differently than the convenience store clerk who punches in their daily lottery numbers.

College Athletes Are Already Paid in Full

But let me get back to my primary point. The notion that a full scholarship isn't a fair exchange for athletic services pro-vided to a university—regardless of how much money an athletic department generates from those services—is ridiculous. As a former, low-level Division I football player, I can say with a clear conscience that college athletes are not getting ripped off. Now, they might be allowing themselves to get exploited by not taking advantage of their educational opportunity. But that's within their control.

Do you know what people around the world would be willing to endure for a chance to be educated at one of our institutions of higher learning? Hell, people are dying on makeshift boats damn near every day just trying to sneak over here and live in one of our "slums." And I'm supposed to feel sorry because a university is selling a jersey and not kicking back a few of the dollars to Joe Running Back?

I always thought part of the educational process at college was "the struggle." A kid shouldn't eat McDonald's every day. Some days he should be forced to eat macaroni and cheese because he blew all of his money on beer, pizza and weed over the weekend. And trust me on this, you give a bunch of teenage, wannabe professional athletes a stipend and a significant portion of that money will be going directly

Athletic Scholarships Undermine Higher Education

In 1953, ironically the same year that NCAA executive director Walter Byers invented the term *student-athlete*, the association approved athletic scholarships across the board. For many people within higher education, this marked a crucial moment in the history of intercollegiate athletics: the shift from amateurism to professionalism.

The Ivy League, the founders of big-time college sports, responded by refusing to give athletic scholarships and continuing their policy of need-based-only aid to all students, including athletes. They also began to deemphasize their college sports programs in various ways, including prohibiting their teams from playing in bowl games and not allowing spring football practice. Their moves sharpened the line between college sports amateurism and professionalism.

On the Ivy side, and also at the schools that joined them and eventually formed NCAA Division III, were teams with players who were authentic students at their colleges and universities. On the other side were all the schools awarding athletic scholarships and hoping that their athletes could pass their institution's educational requirements; but if the jocks failed academically, the schools would accommodate them, including with "gut" courses and "mickey" majors. As a result, the higher education landscape divided between big-time college sports schools, and academic colleges and universities. A minority of institutions managed to straddle the line, but the majority did not.

From the perspective of the twenty-first century, it is clear that the Ivy League presidents and Boards of Trustees came to a fork in the higher education road and had to choose between big-time college sports or big-time undergraduate education. They chose the academic path, and this decision helped the Ivy League ascend to the pinnacle of American higher education. Other schools selected the other path and began the slow but inevitable degradation of undergraduate education at their institutions.

Murray Sperber, *Beer and Circus: How Big-Time College Sports Is Crippling Undergraduate Education.* New York: Henry Holt, 2000.

to the local "pharmacist" for steroids and marijuana, another good chunk will get guzzled down a beer bong and the rest will be a down payment on a platinum necklace, just like the one Lil Wayne wore in his last video.

You can get mad at me if you want to and accuse me of a gross generalization, but I lived it. I've seen it with my own eyes. I've driven athletes to the shopping mall and watched them buy Air Jordans and the Run DMC dookie gold chain with their Pell Grant money. College athletes don't need movie and laundry money. They need to be slapped back into reality. People need to tell them just how good they've got it. We need to stress to them that the educational opportunity they've been afforded is more valuable than the "pocket money" an Ed Martin can provide.

We need to share the uniquely American story about five black boys who carried a bumbling coach, an entire athletic department, a local community and the NCAA to unprecedented riches and 10 years later found their biggest star indicted for perjury and their biggest booster facing four years in jail. All because they believed the hype that college basketball owed them more than an education.

"African American male student-athletes are excluded disproportionately as a result of the initial eligibility requirements."

College Entrance Requirements for Athletes Are Unfair

Robert M. Sellers, Tabbye M. Chavous, and Tony N. Brown

Robert M. Sellers and Tabbye M. Chavous are professors of psychology at the University of Michigan, and Tony N. Brown is a professor of sociology at Vanderbilt University. In the following viewpoint they criticize the National Collegiate Athletic Association's initial eligibility requirements, which require high school students to have a certain minimum grade point average and SAT score in order to qualify for an athletic scholarship. These requirements have resulted in fewer black students receiving athletic scholarships. The NCAA implemented these requirements, write the authors, in the belief that they would motivate high school students to do better academically. However, the authors contend that African American student athletes generally have worse academic records not because they are unmotivated but because many of them come from poor neighborhoods where high schools have little funding.

As you read, consider the following questions:

1. When were Propositions 48, 42, and 16 first implemented, respectively?
2. What alternative to the initial eligibility requirements for student athletes does the authors propose?

Robert M. Sellers, Tabbye M. Chavous, and Tony N. Brown, "Uneven Playing Field: The Impact of Structural Barriers on the Initial Eligibility of African American Student-Athletes," *Paradoxes of Youth and Sport*, edited by Margaret Gatz, Michael A. Messner, and Sandra J. Ball-Rokeach. Albany: State University of New York Press. Copyright © 2002 by State University of New York Press. All rights reserved. Reproduced by permission.

Historically, sports, along with entertainment, has been one of the few avenues of upward mobility in American society in which African Americans might hope to be judged on their ability instead of their skin color. Although African American males are underrepresented in just about every traditional venue for upward socioeconomic mobility in our society (e.g., education), they are significantly over-represented in professional football, baseball, basketball, and boxing. While African Americans constitute 13% of the population and approximately 9% of the student population at National Collegiate Athletic Association (NCAA) Division I institutions (the most competitive level), they constitute about 25% of the student-athletes who are on scholarships at these institutions. Approximately 1 of every 9 African American males on the campuses of the 302 Division I universities are scholarship athletes. In contrast, only 1 of every 50 White male college students are scholarship athletes. Intercollegiate athletics clearly has become an important vehicle for higher educational attainment among African American males.

The Reform Movement in Intercollegiate Athletics

Over the past fifteen years, the approximately 300-member institutions that comprise the NCAA's Division I have been engaged in a reform movement to restore academic integrity to intercollegiate athletics. The reform movement has been influenced, in part, by embarrassing and tragic incidents that left big-time college athletics with a major image problem. Much of the focus of the NCAA's reform efforts has been directed toward making incoming student-athletes as similar academically to the rest of the student body as possible by increasing the precollege academic requirements for the initial eligibility of potential students. As a result, Proposition 48 was implemented in the fall of 1986. The legislation required that potential student-athletes obtain a high school grade point average (GPA) of 2.0 in a set of core courses as well as at least a 700 combined score on the SAT to be eligible to participate in athletics during their first year. A potential student-athlete who met only one of the requirements was considered a partial qualifier and was ruled ineligible to compete during their first year. However, the partial qualifier was allowed to receive an athletic scholarship. In 1989, the NCAA passed Proposition 42 that eliminated the partial qualifier. This legislation meant that all student-athletes must meet both the SAT requirement and the grade point average or they would lose the opportunity to receive an athletic scholarship their first year in college as well as lose a year of athletic eligibility. In 1996, the initial eligibility requirements were raised, and a sliding scale was implemented to address some of the criticism levied against the use of a single cutoff score for the SAT. Proposition 16 requires a potential student-athlete with a 2.0 high school core GPA to earn a combined score of 1,010 on the recentered SAT in order to be eligible to receive an athletic scholarship. A potential student-athlete with a combined 820 recentered SAT score (equivalent to 700 on the original SAT) needs at least a 2.5 GPA in 13 core courses in order to be eligible. . . .

There is growing evidence that African American male student-athletes are excluded disproportionately as a result of the initial eligibility requirements. African American athletes enrolled before 1986 were six times more likely than White student-athletes to fail to meet Proposition 48. Approximately 65% of the African American athletes who entered before Proposition 42 standards came into effect in 1990 would have been ineligible under those standards. Meanwhile, only 9% of the White male and female athletes would have suffered the same fate. A 1993 NCAA report reveals that the percentage of African American male freshman athletes dropped significantly in the year immediately following the implementation of Proposition 48. Although the percentages of African American male athletes steadily increased over the next two years, they still did not reach the percentages witnessed in the pre–Proposition 48 year of 1984.

Other studies have reported evidence suggesting that many of the African American student-athletes who are excluded from full participation and scholarship opportunities by the initial eligibility requirements would actually graduate if they are given the chance. The NCAA reported findings regarding the graduation class of 1984, two years before

Proposition 48 went into effect, that 54% of African American male athletes who attended and subsequently graduated from the surveyed institutions would have been disqualified from freshman eligibility by the standardized test requirement of Proposition 48. Similarly, [a 1987 study] reported that 60% of the African American football players at the University of Michigan from 1974 to 1983 would not have been eligible under Propositions 48 and 42. Yet, 87% of those African American football players who would have been excluded under Propositions 48 and 42 actually graduated.

The Motivational Argument

The NCAA reform movement's focus on increasing initial eligibility requirements has been based on the idea that the academic problems of student-athletes are motivational in nature. Four major assumptions underlie this motivation argument: (1) a large number of athletes undervalue academic achievement; (2) academic motivation is related to academic achievement for athletes; (3) taking away athletic opportunities will motivate student-athletes to work harder in the classroom; and (4) high schools are not motivated to prepare athletes academically, because there is no consequence for them not doing so. Specifically, the assumption has been that too many student-athletes place too much emphasis on athletics and not enough emphasis on academics. Thus, it is believed that the higher eligibility standards send the message to potential student-athletes in junior high school and high school that they must place a greater emphasis on academics if they plan to play sports in college. Furthermore, it is presumed that potential student-athletes' improved academic preparation at the secondary level will result in increases in the graduation rates once they reach college. Finally, some proponents believe that the initial eligibility requirements will send a message to high schools that they also must do a better job of preparing their athletes for the rigors of college work. The potential rejection of their underprepared athletes, therefore, will motivate schools to better prepare athletes academically.

With respect to the first assumption of the motivation argument, the research literature contradicts the premise that a significant number of student-athletes undervalue academics. In 1986, the NCAA commissioned the American Institutes for Research (AIR) to survey student-athletes at 42 Division I institutions about their academic, athletic, and social experiences. Overall, 95% of the student-athletes in football and basketball reported that getting a college degree was either important or of the greatest importance to them. In a report written specifically about African American athletes, AIR states that more than 82% of African American basketball and football players reported getting a college degree as being of the greatest importance. In both instances, student-athletes' reports of the importance of obtaining a degree were not significantly different from those of a comparison sample of college students who did not participate in intercollegiate athletics. . . .

In addition to focusing on the personal motivation of the student-athlete, the motivation argument also assumes that initial eligibility requirements will somehow boost the high

Poorer Black Students Hardest Hit by Initial Eligibility Rules

Percentage of African American and White
Recruited Applicants to the NCAA Clearinghouse
in 1997 by Self-Reported Family Income

	% of African American Applicants	% of African American Ineligible	% of White Applicants	% of White Ineligible
Greater than $80,000	9.3	9.2	31.8	2.1
$50,000 to $79,999	17.7	14.2	29.3	3.5
$30,000 to $49,000	23.5	20.1	18.8	6.6
Less than $30,000	37.3	27.8	8.5	8.9
Missing	12.2	24.4	11.6	4.3
Total	100.0	21.4	100.0	4.2

Note: African Americans constitute 14.1% and whites constitute 69.5% of the applicant pool.

Robert M. Sellers, Tabbye M. Chavous, and Tony N. Brown, "Uneven Playing Field: The Impact of Structural Barriers on the Initial Eligibility of African American Student-Athletes," in Margaret Gatz, Michael A. Messner, and Sandra J. Ball-Rokeach, eds., *Paradoxes of Youth and Sport.* Albany: State University of New York Press, 2002.

schools' motivation to better prepare their athletes academically. The NCAA, of course, has neither funding nor regulatory powers over high schools. Yet, implicit in this final assumption of the motivation argument is the belief that high schools have the capacity to do a better job of preparing athletes but, for whatever reasons, are not motivated to do so. At present, there is no empirical evidence to support such an argument. Moreover, such a claim is simply illogical. If high schools are not already motivated to prepare their students as well as they possibly can, then it is doubtful that punishing these very same students by denying them access to an athletic scholarship will motivate the high schools. Furthermore, the school level factors that have been related to high school academic performance (e.g., classroom size) do not suggest student motivation issues, but, rather, are tied to the level at which schools are funded.

In summary, student-athletes on average come to college less prepared than other nonathletic students. African American athletes come from poorer educational backgrounds than their White counterparts and once in college, they perform less well academically. The motivation argument would suggest that these differences in academic preparation are, in part, a function of differences in motivation. In essence, African American male student-athletes must suffer from lower academic aspirations or place less effort into their studies than their White counterparts. Interestingly, Sellers found no race differences in either aspirations or the amount of effort that student-athletes place on their schoolwork.

An Alternative Argument: The Structural Barrier Argument

A structural barrier argument may help explain the differences between the academic performance of African American collegiate athletes and White college athletes more accurately than the assumptions underlying the current motivation argument. The structural barrier argument suggests that those academic differences are a function of the *quality* of the educational experiences available to African American and White student-athletes at the secondary level. The quality of the public education available to a child in the

United States varies greatly and is a function of the financial status of that child's family. People who live in communities that are more affluent have a greater tax base from which to finance their public schools and, thus, have more money spent on their children's public education. . . .

A structural barrier argument would suggest that there are two main factors that have caused African American student-athletes to be affected disproportionately by the increased initial eligibility requirements. First, athletics has historically been and continues to be one of the most visible avenues for African American students from poor backgrounds to achieve upward mobility. Thus, athletics plays a much different role in the lives of poor African Americans than in any other group (including more affluent African Americans). Second, African Americans are overrepresented among the poor. As a result, African American student-athletes are the sole representatives on our college campuses of a growing number of African American high school students who, because they are not athletically gifted and are trapped in a deplorable educational system, have less access to higher education. For most such students, a college education is not a viable option.

African American student-athletes often come from different high schools and significantly poorer socioeconomic and educational backgrounds than even their African American nonathletic college classmates. Such differences are related to different admissions processes for the two groups. The football team and the admissions office do not recruit from the same place. The admissions office recruits African American students from schools that have strong academic reputations and whose graduates go on to college. Often, these schools have a disproportionately high number of African Americans from the upper levels of the socioeconomic stratum. Meanwhile, the football coach recruits from any school that has athletes with athletic talent. Since there is no evidence that athletic ability is causally related to socioeconomic status, the football team—more than the rest of the African Americans on campus—is representative of the African American population in terms of socioeconomic level. Unfortunately, many students from the same poor educational environment who do not possess superior athletic ability, but who have performed better academically than their athletic classmates, do not get the same opportunity for a higher education. Thus, excellence in athletics becomes one of the few keys that will open the door to higher education. As a result, African American student-athletes are often the only representatives of the inner-city educational system on many of the campuses of our most elite institutions of higher education. . . .

Help Student-Athletes Rather than Rejecting Them

Member institutions of the NCAA would be better served if they focused more of their efforts on improving student-athletes' educational opportunities once they are on-campus, instead of focusing on their selection of student-athletes. The fact that African American athletes historically have and continue to graduate at rates higher than African American nonathletes despite coming to college with lower test scores and high school GPAs, suggests the possibility of effective intervention aimed at the student-athletes' experiences once they are on campus. . . .

In many ways, the issues surrounding the initial eligibility of African American student-athletes mirror those that face our educational system in general. In both instances, there is a tension between issues of personal responsibility and structural inequities as primary causal forces in students' academic performance. With respect to intercollegiate athletics, it is clear that both advocates of the motivational argument and the structural barrier argument would agree that significant reform is needed. As such, intercollegiate athletics is uniquely situated to provide innovative solutions to what may be the major dilemma of higher education in the next century: the problem of striving for academic excellence while at the same time providing equal access to all citizens. One thing is certain regarding the NCAA's reform efforts. The elementary and secondary educational playing field is not level. Hence, any reform effort that targets student-athletes' motivation without also addressing structural inequities in our education system is destined to exacerbate those inequities.

"The notion that poor black kids are being denied opportunities . . . is nonsense."

College Entrance Requirements for Athletes Are Fair

David Goldfield

David Goldfield is a professor of history at the University of North Carolina and a member of the Initial Eligibility Committee of the National Collegiate Athletic Association. In the following viewpoint he defends an NCAA rule known as Proposition 16, which requires student athletes to meet certain minimum academic standards in order to be eligible for athletic scholarships. In March 1999 a federal court ruled that Proposition 16 was discriminatory, since it would result in more black than white students becoming ineligible for athletic scholarships. Writing in April 1999, Goldfield deplores the court ruling and argues that weakening the NCAA's student-athlete eligibility requirements will ultimately harm blacks. He contends that the eligibility requirement was first implemented to prevent schools from admitting unqualified black applicants, exploiting them for their athletic ability, and then not graduating them. The best solution, in his view, is to improve the quality of secondary education in black communities.

As you read, consider the following questions:

1. What percent of black athletes applying for scholarships were ineligible in 1998, according to the author?
2. What trend in inner-city schools does Goldfield cite as a reason for keeping minimum scores on standardized tests as part of the NCAA's eligibility requirements?

David Goldfield, "Weaker NCAA Standards Won't Help Black Athletes," *Chronicle of Higher Education*, vol. 45, April 9, 1999, p. A64. Copyright © 1999 by the *Chronicle of Higher Education*. Reproduced by permission.

The . . . federal-court ruling barring the National Collegiate Athletic Association from using Proposition 16, its rule setting academic standards for freshman eligibility, underscores the Hamlet-like strategy that the association pursued in connection with the case. The N.C.A.A. couldn't seem to decide how it felt about academic standards, and therefore sent the court mixed messages on Proposition 16. In effect, the association left it to the judge to sort out its ambivalence.

[In March 1999], in *Cureton et al. v. N.C.A.A.*, Judge Ronald L. Buckwalter ruled that the minimum score on standardized tests that the N.C.A.A. had set for prospective athletes was not based on sound research and was racially discriminatory. . . .

[Since 1997], the N.C.A.A. has been considering its own changes in the eligibility rules, and I have been a member of a five-person committee charged with reviewing Proposition 16. We undertook the task at the request of our Division I Board of Directors, which is composed of 15 university presidents. They, and we as well, wanted to at least maintain—if not increase—the graduation rates of athletes, while at the same time to insure access to higher education for members of minority groups. To that end, our research staff generated data and models to analyze trends in college athletics, and we surveyed faculty members, athletics directors, and presidents at all Division I institutions. Three patterns have emerged.

Each Year More Blacks Meet the Eligibility Requirements

First, the adverse impact of Proposition 16 on African-American athletes has been declining since the proposition, which was adopted in 1992, took effect in 1996. In 1996, 27.3 per cent of black athletes applying for athletics scholarships at colleges and universities, and indicating that they wanted to play intercollegiate sports their freshman year, were ineligible; by 1998, the proportion had declined to 20.6 per cent. The downward trend is consistent with what happened when earlier changes in academic standards were instituted.

Second, since the inauguration of academic standards in the 1980s, graduation rates for all athletes have risen. Projections are that, once the first class admitted under Proposition 16 graduates in 2001, those rates will increase even more. Over all, our committee concluded that the N.C.A.A.'s reliance on a student's high-school grade-point average, taken together with standardized-test scores, is the best predictor of college success.

Third, we found that, in the majority of the institutions we surveyed, entering athletes were academically better prepared than they were before Proposition 16 went into effect, and did better in their classes. And that has been achieved without any noticeable decline in athletic performance. The majority of our respondents thus favored retaining the current academic standards. Only a small minority (9.1 per cent) supported removing a minimum score on standardized tests from the criteria for initial eligibility.

The Importance of Standardized Tests

Yet, from the beginning of our deliberations, the N.C.A.A. leadership has encouraged us to eliminate the test-score minimum. [In 1998], the N.C.A.A. president, Cedric W. Dempsey, stated in a widely reported speech that Proposition 16 should be modified. He was not the only association official to make such comments. The N.C.A.A.'s Research Committee—which is responsible for carrying out studies, but not for recommending policy—took the unprecedented step last June [1998] of calling for the abolition of the requirement of a minimum score on standardized tests. Small wonder that Judge Buckwalter noted in his opinion that the N.C.A.A.'s legal team "generally disavowed statements made by N.C.A.A. executives as merely personal opinions."

N.C.A.A. officials feared that Proposition 16 could not be defended legally, because it set the minimum test score at slightly more than one standard deviation below the national mean, while it set the minimum G.P.A. at two standard deviations below the national mean. Since black students score lower on standardized tests, on average, than white students, N.C.A.A. officials worried that putting more weight on test scores than on G.P.A. scores appeared discriminatory. The association was also under strong pressure from its own Minority Opportunities and Interests Committee, as well as from several outside black organizations, to lower the test-score standard.

By admitting, in effect, that Proposition 16 is indefensible, the N.C.A.A. handed the court the rationale for ruling against the association.

What some N.C.A.A. officials seemed to ignore was the fact that there are good reasons to weight the standardized-test score more than the G.P.A. For one, grade inflation has increased during the past decade. The proportion of college-bound seniors reporting an A average increased from 28 per cent in 1987 to 37 per cent in 1997, according to a recent book by Michele Hernandez, a former admissions official at Dartmouth College. The trend is particularly apparent in inner-city schools that enroll a large number of minority students: According to a 1994 study by the U.S. Department of Education, students receiving an A-minus in schools in impoverished areas would have probably received a C or a D in schools in more affluent areas.

Rising Student-Athlete Graduation Rates

The following NCAA data shows the percentage graduation rates of students who entered NCAA Division I schools from 1992 through 1996, the year that Proposition 16 eligibility requirements first took effect.

Year students entered	General student body	All student-athletes	Black male student-athletes
1996	59	62	48
1995	59	60	43
1994	56	58	42
1993	56	58	41
1992	56	58	40

National Collegiate Athletic Association, 2003 Graduation Rates Report for NCAA Division I Schools, www.ncaa.org.

There are also reasons to worry about the impact of dropping parts of Proposition 16. If we do away with minimum standardized-test scores, there is no doubt that some athletes who would have been ineligible under the rule will be able to compete as freshmen at Division I institutions, on the basis of their grade-point averages. Indeed, one of the plaintiffs in *Cureton* had achieved a 690 out of 1,600 on the SAT. (She took the test before it was recentered, and ranked near the 14th percentile of test takers—below the N.C.A.A.'s cutoff at that time of 700.) Yet the young woman boasted a 3.5 grade-point average in high school and was fifth in her class. Under Proposition 16, the minimum score required on the recentered SAT is 820, a score that places students in the 17th percentile of test takers. On the ACT, 68 out of 144 is required. Do we really want to admit students who cannot even achieve that standard?

The Charge of Racism

To be sure, we should be concerned about racism, or at least about the significant racial disparities allegedly generated by Proposition 16. But doing away with minimum standardized-test scores doesn't solve anything. Even without using test scores, 15.7 per cent of African-American college athletes in the fall of 1998 would have been declared ineligible, compared with 2.7 per cent of white athletes. In other words, significant racial disparities would have persisted. In fact, if we devise any academic standards worthy of the name, African-American athletes will be disproportionately affected. The only alternative is to do away with standards altogether, but then we would be back in the very position—exploiting minority athletes who are unlikely to succeed in higher education—that resulted in the imposition of academic standards during the 1980s.

The problem lies in the assumption that academic standards unfairly discriminate against African-American athletes. According to Jack McArdle, the head of the N.C.A.A.'s research team, with each passing year since Proposition 16 was put into effect, the number of African-American athletes in Division I institutions has increased (not by a great amount, but enough to indicate an upward trend). While critics point out that the percentage of black athletes among all student athletes has declined, that may be due to the increased emphasis Division I institutions are putting on some sports—such as crew, field hockey, and soccer—in which women, but not always black athletes, participate. Moreover, when the first class admitted under Proposition 16 graduates in 2001, the indications are that graduation rates for all athletes will rise. As Gary R. Roberts, an expert on sports law at the Tulane University School of Law, recently said to me, "The notion that poor black kids are being denied opportunities by Proposition 16 is nonsense." Roberts added, "I only wish that those who are so driven to allow schools to take academically unprepared black athletes would be more concerned about creating educational opportunities for minority students whether or not they play basketball."

Instead, the N.C.A.A. leadership has succumbed to the syndrome of white guilt about black victimization that informs too much of American race relations. That is, black people claim a wrong allegedly caused by racism, and white people tailor policies to address that wrong. Both parties are sincere and mean well, and there is no doubt that racism does exist in society. But we make a tacit bargain that perpetuates African-American inequality. People expect African-American youngsters to continue to perform poorly on standardized tests and—surprise!—they do. What we don't do is make a serious effort to help them improve their scores—and their educational backgrounds.

As the N.C.A.A. considers its strategies for appealing Judge Buckwalter's opinion, I urge its officials to be careful not to weaken eligibility requirements. Doing so will not help black athletes, and it will not help the colleges and universities the association is supposed to represent.

The irony in the current controversy is that, historically, members of minority groups have used standardized tests to overcome discrimination. In 1955, for example, Thurgood Marshall, then a lawyer for the N.A.A.C.P., countered segregationists' arguments that school desegregation would fail because black children were inferior intellectually to whites. Arguing before the U.S. Supreme Court, which was considering how fast to mandate desegregation, Marshall challenged segregated schools to give children of both races standardized tests "and educate them according to test results rather than by the color of their skin."

"Placing legal wagers on games played by young people should not be permitted."

Gambling on College Sports Should Be Banned Nationwide

William S. Saum

William S. Saum is director of agent, gambling, and amateurism activities for the National Collegiate Athletic Association. The following viewpoint is adapted from testimony that Saum gave before the Nevada State Assembly in March 2001. In it he urges Nevada (where gambling is legal) to ban wagering on college sports. Saum maintains that sports betting results in scandals where athletes purposefully lose games or keep the scores close for the benefit of gamblers. Saum also contends that legal sports betting in Nevada is fueling the growth of gambling among college students nationwide. In his view a nationwide ban on college sports wagering would be a major step toward eliminating the negative influence that gambling has on students, young athletes, and the games they play. As of fall 2004, a nationwide ban on college sports wagering had not been enacted.

As you read, consider the following questions:

1. What federal commission recommended a total ban on wagering on college sports?
2. How much money was wagered in Nevada sports books in 2000, according to the viewpoint?
3. What percent of teenagers said they had bet on college sports in the June 1999 Gallup poll cited by Saum?

William S. Saum, testimony before the Judiciary Committee of the Nevada State Assembly, March 2, 2001.

The NCAA [National Collegiate Athletic Association] is a tax-exempt, unincorporated association of approximately 1,150 colleges, universities, athletics conferences and related organizations devoted to the regulation and promotion of intercollegiate athletics for male and female student-athletes. Like many other sports organizations, the NCAA has a clear, direct policy regarding sports wagering. The NCAA prohibits participation in any form of legal or illegal sports wagering because of its potential to undermine the integrity of sports contests and jeopardize the welfare of the student-athlete and the intercollegiate athletics community. The NCAA membership has adopted specific legislation prohibiting athletics department staff members, conference office staff and student-athletes from engaging in sports wagering activities as they relate to intercollegiate or professional sporting events. These same rules apply to NCAA national office staff.

Betting's Effect on Sports and Athletes

As a sports organization, the NCAA is well aware of the direct threat sports wagering poses to the integrity of each intercollegiate contest. In the early 1950's, the academic community and the public were shocked to learn that the City College of New York men's basketball team was involved in a point-shaving scandal. We are all aware of recent point shaving scandals on the campuses of Arizona State University and Northwestern University. The magnitude of these and similar incidents should not be underestimated. According to federal law enforcement officials, more money was wagered in the Arizona State case than on any point-shaving scam in the history of intercollegiate athletics. It is important to note that over $1 million was wagered legally in Nevada casinos in the Arizona State case. Likewise, in the Northwestern case, wagers were placed legally in Nevada casinos.

Both legal and illegal sports wagering have been at the heart of nearly every major collegiate sports wagering scandal. However, the presence of any type of sports wagering whether it be legal or illegal is a potential threat to the integrity of our contests. We believe that eliminating sports wagering will provide important positive benefits for intercollegiate athletics. Nevada casinos have been helpful in monitoring unusual shifts in wagering on college games, but this alone does not ensure protection from point-shaving scandals. In fact, some point-shaving scandals have utilized Las Vegas sports books without being detected. A blanket prohibition on collegiate sports wagering will significantly reduce the outlets available for placing wagers and, in doing so, will undoubtedly have an impact on the number of individuals betting on the games.

The influence of sports wagering is far reaching, and sports organizations continually live in fear that sports wagering will infiltrate and undermine the contest itself.

As director of agent, gambling and amateurism activities, and a former campus administrator and coach, I am acutely aware of the impact sports wagering can have on the lives of college student-athletes. I have witnessed students, their families and institutions publicly humiliated. I have seen students expelled from college, lose athletics scholarships worth thousands of dollars and jeopardize any hope of a professional career in athletics. In most cases, the scenario is strikingly familiar. Student-athletes who have begun wagering on sports incur losses beyond their means to repay and, as a result, become vulnerable to point-shaving schemes. Sometimes they participate in such activities voluntarily in a desperate attempt to erase their outstanding debt; other times, they are compelled by the threat of personal injury. In the latter cases, organized crime is often involved and there are cases where student bookmaking operations can be traced back to organized crime.

The profile of the typical college student who gambles is someone who believes he/she can control his/her own destiny, is willing to take risks and believes that he/she possesses the skill to be successful in this endeavor. In other contexts, these are considered positive character traits. This profile is representative of many college athletes and may, in part, explain why some student-athletes are drawn to sports wagering.

NCAA investigations have revealed that there is a high incidence of wagering among college students. It is believed that student bookies are present at every institution. The advent of Internet wagering, which now enables college students to place wagers over the Internet from their dorm rooms, raises even greater cause for concern. There is certainly no dispute that the impact of sports wagering is being felt on college campuses across the country.

Federal Commission Supports a Ban

On June 18, 1999, the federally appointed National Gambling Impact Study Commission, convened by Congress to examine the effects of sports wagering on American society, issued its final report after a two-year comprehensive study of all forms of legal gambling activity.

The commission's report included a recommendation urging a ban on all currently legal sports wagering on college and amateur sporting events. In making this recommendation, the commission said, "Sports wagering threatens the integrity of sports, it puts student-athletes in a vulnerable position, it can serve as a gateway behavior for adolescent gamblers and it can devastate individuals and careers."

Placing legal wagers on games played by young people should not be permitted. The existence of any type of gambling, illegal or legal, on sporting events is a direct threat to the integrity of the contest. Participants in college sporting events are even more susceptible (than professional athletes) to outside influences who may attempt to exert pressures on them to "fix" the outcome of a contest. The development of new gambling technologies, such as programs designed to allow casino bettors to wager on each individual play in a game, will undoubtedly increase the likelihood that college student-athletes will be pressured and enticed into schemes where they participate in influencing the outcome of a given college sporting contest. We must remember that these are young people; betting on their performance is unseemly and inappropriate.

The legally and illegally wagered dollars on college sporting events are thought to be in the billions. Complicating the matter is the money laundering of illegal sports book dollars through legal sports books. Steve DuCharme, former chair of the Nevada Gaming Control Board, is quoted in a February 1999, *Sports Business Journal* article as saying:

> "We've taken steps to crack down on the amount of illegal money being laundered through legitimate sports books. We really have no way of knowing [how much is laundered

through the legal sports books]. Based on transcriptions of wiretaps, it is millions of dollars."

These are clearly federal law enforcement issues, meriting a federal solution.

The Nevada Economy

Fears that federal legislation prohibiting sports wagering in Nevada will be a "serious threat" to the Nevada economy are not supported by the facts. In 2000, approximately $2.3 billion was wagered in Nevada sports books. Casinos retained $124 million, approximately 5.33 percent of the total amount wagered on sports. According to Mr. DuCharme, the amount kept by casinos on sports wagering is "very small" compared to other casino games. Furthermore, the amount wagered on college sports is only a little more than one-third of the total. In an industry driven by billions of dollars (2000 total casino revenues were $9.6 billion), the elimination of collegiate sports wagering will have little impact on state revenues or on the casinos' bottom line. The amount bet on college sports is reportedly only four-tenths of one percent of overall casino revenues.

The existence of legal sports wagering in Nevada is actually limiting the growth of the Nevada economy in some regards. Most amateur and professional sports leagues have policies against franchise location and events staged in Nevada because of the presence of sports wagering.

Gambling Among Youth

We are concerned that legal collegiate sports wagering fuels a much larger illegal collegiate sports wagering trade, impacting America's youth at an alarming rate. Sports wagering is a serious problem among teenagers under the age of 18. A 1999 Gallup Poll reports that teenagers say they start betting on college sports at age 10 and bet on college sports at twice the rate of adults. Called "the addiction of the 90's" by the American Academy of Pediatrics, their research indicates that there are over one million United States teens who are addicted to gambling. A recent Harvard School of Medicine report estimates that six percent of teenagers under 18 have serious gambling problems. In a June report of the 1999 Gallup

Poll, 18 percent of teenage respondents said they had bet on college sports, contrasted with nine percent of adults who wagered on college games. The National Gambling Impact Study Commission report calls sports wagering "a gateway behavior for adolescent gamblers." Prohibiting college sports wagering everywhere in the United States would send a clear signal that the activity is illegal. In addition, a federal prohibition would put an end to the mixed message to our young people, limit exposure and reduce the numbers of people who are introduced to sports wagering.

College Sports Betting Scandals of the 1990s

Nevada casinos now reap close to $1,000,000,000 a year in wagers on college football and basketball games.

This bonanza for Nevada wagering establishments comes at a tremendous price to our colleges and universities—and to the athletes themselves. According to National Collegiate Athletic Association president Cedric Dempsey, "The millions of dollars wagered legally on college sports has resulted in more 'point-shaving' and 'game-fixing' scandals in the 1990s than the previous five decades combined." Those scandals have ensnared dozens of athletes from some of the nation's most prestigious academic institutions:

• At Northwestern University, 11 student-athletes were convicted in gambling scandals involving the school's athletic teams. Among them were the football team's star tailback, Dennis Lundy, who admitted to intentionally fumbling the ball at the goal line in a 1994 game against the University of Iowa so he could win a bet. Two Northwestern basketball players were convicted of trying to fix three games in exchange for bribes from gamblers.

• Thirteen members of the Boston College football team were suspended for gambling in 1996, including two who bet against the Eagles.

• The all-time leading passer at the University of Maryland, Scott Milanovich, was suspended for four games in 1995 for betting on college sports.

• Arizona State All-America point guard Stevin ("Hedake") Smith sacrificed a promising pro basketball career and ended up in prison after he and a teammate were found guilty of shaving points during the 1993–94 season.

James C. Dobson, "Gambling with the Future of College Sports," *USA Today Magazine*, May 2001.

The NCAA has taken significant steps to address the very real problems associated with wagering on college sports. The NCAA has established policies that prohibit all sports wagering by campus athletics personnel, student-athletes and NCAA employees. Student-athletes are not eligible to compete if they knowingly provide information to individuals involved in organized gambling activities concerning intercollegiate athletics competition; solicit a bet on any intercollegiate team; accept a bet on any intercollegiate team; accept a bet on any team representing the institution or participate in any gambling activity that involves intercollegiate athletics through a bookmaker, parlay card or any other method employed by organized gambling. Similar expectations apply to coaches, directors of athletics and NCAA employees. Recently, the NCAA instituted background checks on men's and women's basketball game officials. This was done to ensure that the game officials have not been involved in sports wagering issues. In addition, the NCAA sponsors the following: educational programs that provide assistance to campus administrators to conduct sports wagering workshops, broadcasts of anti–sports wagering public service announcements during the championship games aired by CBS and ESPN, production of a booklet in partnership with the National Endowment for Financial Education entitled "Don't Bet On It," which educates students about the dangers of sports wagering and acquaints them with good financial management strategies. We are also currently working to develop research in the area of youth gambling and campus gambling.

Safeguarding the Integrity of College Sports

Opponents of an effort to prohibit gambling on college sports in all states criticize the NCAA for reaping profits from college sports while not investing more in gambling prevention programs. As previously mentioned, the NCAA supports a number of programs that address the sports wagering issue. In addition, a portion of the NCAA's revenues fund programs such as the student-athlete assistance fund, graduate assistance fellowships, life skills education, clinics for disadvantaged youth, and many other programs designed to support and enrich the college experience for student-athletes. The NCAA's 84 championship events for men and women at the Divisions I, II and III levels are funded through the television rights revenues. However, the vast majority of NCAA revenues are returned to NCAA Divisions I, II and III member colleges and universities to help support their athletics programs. It costs $3.4 billion every year for our member schools to provide the more than 335,000 student-athletes with an opportunity to play college sports. The NCAA and its member institutions continue to examine ways to provide student-athletes with more support and enrichment opportunities, including gambling-related education, research and outreach activities.

Legalized amateur sports wagering in Nevada continues to blunt efforts of the NCAA and higher education to combat college sports wagering. The insidious effect of legalized wagering on college sports has crept far beyond the Nevada state line. Even though sports wagering is illegal in nearly every state, point spreads on college games are published in newspapers across the country, bookies are common fixtures on college campuses and new technologies allow bets on college games to be placed over the Internet or in a casino in innovative ways. The dollars involved are big and escalating every year. By clearly making gambling on college sports illegal everywhere all the time, we will strengthen our efforts to maintain the integrity of college sports.

This nation's college and university system is one of our greatest assets. We offer the world the model for postsecondary education. Betting on the outcome of college sporting events tarnishes the integrity of sport and diminishes the esteem in which we and the rest of the world hold United States colleges and universities. While we recognize that a ban on collegiate sports wagering will not eliminate all gambling on college sports, it is a significant start. Our goal is to protect student-athletes and remove the unseemly influences of sports wagering on our amateur athletes and the games they play. We look forward to working with you to close the gap that has not only allowed legal betting on college sports to continue but also fuels illegal betting on college games.

"There is no persuasive evidence that legal sports betting in Nevada is responsible for the betting scandals and illegal gambling everywhere else."

Gambling on College Sports Should Not Be Banned Nationwide

Danny Sheridan

Betting on college sports is illegal in every state except Nevada. In the following viewpoint, Danny Sheridan argues against congressional legislation intended to extend the ban nationwide. He contends that such a measure will do nothing to combat the illegal wagering that is taking place across the country. However, in Nevada it will drive betting on college sports underground and out of the reach of regulators, who currently monitor the industry for game fixing and other forms of corruption. Sheridan is a sports analyst and the author of several books on sports betting. As of fall 2004, betting on college sports remained legal in Nevada.

As you read, consider the following questions:

1. What percentage of sports gambling is done illegally, according to Sheridan?
2. What examples does the author cite to illustrate his point that gambling is part of American culture?
3. What mixed message does the proposed legislation to ban college sports betting send, in Sheridan's opinion?

Danny Sheridan, testimony before the Senate Commerce Committee, Washington, DC, April 26, 2001.

My name is Danny Sheridan, and I have been involved with sports and the sports promotion business for more than 25 years. I have published college and pro football magazines, written about sports in a variety of national publications, and have been the host of a number of sports TV and radio shows. I am a lifelong resident of Mobile, Alabama, and a graduate of the University of Alabama School of Business.

I have written exclusively for *USA Today* since its inception in 1982. For *USA Today*, I set the daily odds on every sport along with political and esoteric odds—for example, will Alan Greenspan lower the interest rate, and if so, by how much. My sports and political predictions have been featured on every major network and nearly every major newspaper and radio station in the country. I plan to continue setting these odds and providing them to *USA Today* even if this legislation [the Amateur Sports Integrity Act] is passed.

However, I'm not just a sports—and sometimes political—analyst. I am friends with many high profile college and NFL coaches as well as many NFL and NBA owners. I have spoken at or visited most of the colleges and universities in the United States, and have talked to thousands of students about their concerns about sports betting on their campuses. I've also interviewed many of the world's biggest legal, illegal, and offshore bookmakers.

I'm sure there are a lot of people brighter than me at this hearing; however, I'm confident in saying that my predictions, contacts and knowledge of the sports world would stack up against anyone in this room.

That's why I'm here today.

I do not bet on sports, don't smoke or drink alcohol, but I do recognize, like you, that in a free society people do these things, sometimes to excess.

Legal Betting Is Not the Problem

I commend you for having the courage to take on the tough issue of fighting illegal gambling. However, I want to warn you of the serious, unintended, and adverse consequences that will surely result from the passage and implementation of this legislation. Your attempt to eliminate legal college sports wagering—while well intentioned—would only result in an increase in illegal college sports gambling and an increase in the amount of fixing and point shaving schemes and scandals.

Currently, approximately 99 percent of all sports gambling takes place illegally outside of Nevada. In 1999, the National Gambling Impact Study Commission estimated that illegal sports wagering was as much as $380 billion—but I think that it's higher. An estimated 40 million Americans currently wager $6 billion illegally every weekend during the entire 20-week college and pro football season alone.

Comparatively, legal and regulated sports wagering in Nevada is only 1 percent—a tiny fraction—of all of the betting that occurs on sports in this country. And of the approximately $2.3 billion that is legally wagered in Nevada, only about one-third—an even smaller percentage—is bet on college sports.

These figures just show that there is no persuasive evidence that legal sports betting in Nevada is responsible for the betting scandals and illegal gambling everywhere else.

Ban Will Eliminate Oversight

Nevada's legal sports books serve as a legal watchdog for college sports. The point shaving scandals 5 years ago surfaced only because there is a legal authority that exists to watch over the game and betting activity. So in essence, the proposed legislation would remove the only viable enforcement mechanism to monitor and report the fixing of college sports games.

If you take college sports wagering out of Nevada, 100 percent of all NCAA betting would go on illegally. The Nevada Gaming Commission has an incentive to report the fixing of games and to continue to police sports betting to ensure that it's clean. It is legally required to monitor and report suspicious activity, and has done an excellent job monitoring college sports betting. But if you get rid of legal college sports wagering, a person who wants to fix a game will no longer have to worry about the Nevada Gaming Commission, but only about the bookie he placed the bet with and the players involved.

A Ban Would Do Nothing

The gaming industry is among those supporting comprehensive legislation that would increase enforcement and penalties, evaluate the extent and causes of illegal gambling, and require schools to put in place education programs for their students. By contrast, the NCAA is advocating a constitutionally questionable federal ban on legal college sports wagering in Nevada. Despite the NCAA's unsubstantiated claims, its proposal would do nothing to eliminate the widespread illegal gambling occurring on college campuses and elsewhere in this country.

American Gaming Association, "Sports Wagering: An Issue Overview," 2003.

The proposed legislation would make it impossible to monitor and report the fixing of games. The effect of this legislation would be like removing the Securities and Exchange Commission (SEC) from monitoring and policing the stock market. Does the SEC prevent all insider trading? Of course not, but it lets would be criminals know that they'll be prosecuted. In Nevada, you can't bet on a college game through a dummy corporation—you have to do so in person and be 21 or over—and most people know if you fix a sporting event, you'll eventually get caught and prosecuted.

Gambling Is Mainstream Recreation

The NCAA and its supporters also argue that legal betting in Nevada sends a mixed message about gambling to young people. But I'm not sure what mixed message they are talking about.

Gambling and betting is a widely accepted form of recreation in this country and has been an integral part of our history. When our founding fathers needed money to finance the American Revolution, they held a lottery. Today, 47 states permit lotteries, horse and dog racing, commercial and Indian casinos, and/or video poker. Only Hawaii, Utah, and Tennessee have no form of legalized gambling. Since our culture sends the message that gambling is mainstream recreation, it will only make matters worse to deal with illegal sports gambling by making it illegal in Nevada, the one state where these activities are legal and closely monitored.

Finally, it's simply not reasonable to assume that the impulse to gamble can be controlled or reduced by legislation, particularly in this age of Internet gambling, which allows anyone to bet through an offshore sports betting site or casino or both just by the flick of a key on their computer.

Sending a Scary Message

So yes, the passage of this legislation would send a clear message to this country's young people. That message is: We want to cut down on sports gambling and game-fixing so let's ignore the real problem and the impact this legislation would have on college sports. Now that is a scary mixed message.

Again, I believe that the NCAA and its supporters are well intentioned and are only trying to do the best to protect students and college sports. But the idea that Nevada is to blame for the spread of illegal gambling in this country is preposterous. If the NCAA and its proponents think that the passage of this legislation would have any effect on illegal college sports wagering—by young people or adults—they are completely wrong.

Finally, *opposing* this legislation goes *against* my financial interests. If it were to pass, it would benefit me financially. I also have no financial interest in any casinos or Nevada-dependent companies. With this in mind, I hope that this also shows you that my testimony is unbiased and honest.

So I leave you with these odds and a prediction: pass this legislation and I am 100 percent certain that there will be an increase in game fixing and other point shaving schemes and major college sports scandals—exactly the opposite from what I know you are trying to accomplish.

Periodical Bibliography

The following articles have been selected to supplement the diverse views presented in this chapter.

Black Issues in Higher Education	"New Game Plan," April 15, 1999.
Bill Brubaker	"Minimum Standard, Maximum Dispute: Freshman Eligibility Rule Has a Controversial Past and Faces Uncertain Future," *Washington Post*, July 25, 1999.
James C. Dobson	"Gambling with the Future of College Sports," *USA Today Magazine*, May 2001.
Patrick Hruby	"All Bets Off," *Insight on the News*, November 20, 2000.
David Lagesse	"Troubleshooting," *U.S. News & World Report*, March 18, 2002.
David Meggyesy	"Athletes in Big-Time College Sport," *Society*, March/April 2000.
Stephen Moore	"Pointless: College Basketball Players Throw the Game. So What?" *National Review*, December 21, 1998.
New Republic	"March Madness," March 29, 1999.
Ronal Roach	"Academics and Athletics," *Black Issues in Higher Education*, April 8, 2004.
Skip Rozen	"A Whole New Ball Game? The Push to Reform—and Scale Back—Collegiate Athletics Is Gaining Yardage," *Business Week*, October 20, 2003.
William S. Saum	"Sports Gambling in College: Cracking Down on Illegal Betting," *USA Today Magazine*, July 1999.
Welch Suggs	"Athletes' Graduation Rates Set a Record," *Chronicle of Higher Education*, September 12, 2003.
Time	"Throwing the Game," September 25, 2000.
U.S. News & World Report	"Graduation Blues," March 18, 2002.
Arnie Wexler and Mark Isenberg	"Blowing the Whistle on Campus Gambling," *Chronicle of Higher Education*, February 22, 2002.

CHAPTER 3

Is Discrimination a Problem in Sports?

Chapter Preface

The *Racial and Gender Report Card* is an annual report published by the Institute for Diversity and Ethics in Sport at the University of Central Florida (prior to 2002, it was published by Northeastern University's Center for Sport in Society). The report card analyzes the hiring rates of women and people of color in the NBA, NFL, Major League Baseball, NHL, Major League Soccer, the WNBA, and the NCAA and its member institutions.

From its first publication in 1989, the *Report Card* found incremental gains for women and minorities in every sport through 2001. However, the 2003 *Report Card* documents an overall two-year decline in diversity within sports. Every professional sport covered in the report had lower averages for employing women in 2003. Black men continued a decade-long decline in college and professional sports other than basketball. Only the NBA and the NHL improved their minority hiring practices, according to the report.

A major finding of the report is that minorities lost ground in most of the top management positions in college and professional sports, including general managers, team vice presidents, and college athletic directors. Although relatively large numbers of minorities are professional athletes, the major sports leagues have long been dominated by white owners and white management.

Not all of the 2003 *Report Card*'s findings were negative. Perhaps the biggest news was that Black Entertainment Television founder Robert Johnson purchased the Charlotte Sting of the NBA, becoming the first black majority owner in professional sports. There was also an all-time high of twenty-four minority head coaches and managers in the three biggest professional leagues in 2003.

The treatment of minority athletes, particularly black athletes, has been an issue in sports for decades. In the new millennium, the focus is shifting to the representation of minorities in sports management as well as to the continuing underrepresentation of women in sports. In the following chapter the authors debate whether discrimination is a problem in sports.

*"If today's athletes do not strongly state
their feelings on the lack of opportunities
being presented to coaches of color, they will
find . . . doors [slamming] in their faces."*

Minority Coaches Face Discrimination in Hiring

New York Amsterdam News

Although four black men have been hired as head coaches in
the National Football League since the following viewpoint
by the *New York Amsterdam News* was written, controversy
still rages over hiring discrimination in sports. As the *New
York Amsterdam News* points out, the NFL is filled with black
players, many of whom would seem to be excellent candidates for head coaching positions, yet blacks in the coaching
ranks are few. The newspaper contends that black players
and the media should speak out about discrimination in hiring. The *New York Amsterdam News* is a weekly newspaper
that covers news for the African American community.

As you read, consider the following questions:

1. How many coaches in 1997 were black, according to the
   New York Amsterdam News?
2. According to one black assistant coach quoted in the
   viewpoint, what is the "It's my bat and ball syndrome"?
3. What role does the media play in the hiring of minority
   coaches, in the author's view?

It's time for the National Football League (NFL) to give Black coaches opportunity.

The NFL head coaching roulette wheel has spun around several times during early 1997 and not once has it landed on black.[1] This is an injustice that must be addressed by team owners and commissioner Paul Tagliabue's office.

The "Old Boys" Network

The National Football League began its 77th season in 1997. There are 30 head coaching positions in a game that Black athletes predominate. Yet only three teams currently have African Americans as their top man: Dennis Green (Minnesota Vikings), Tony Dungy (Tampa Bay Buccaneers), and Ray Rhodes (Philadelphia Eagles).

Eleven franchises have hired new head coaches, including the New York Jets, the New York Giants and the San Francisco 49ers. None of them gave any serious consideration to deserving men like Sherman Lewis, the Green Bay Packers' offensive coordinator, Emmitt Thomas, the Philadelphia Eagles' defensive coordinator, or Art Shell, the erstwhile head coach of the Los Angeles Raiders.

Instead, the "old boys" network called upon some of its retreads to fill the vacancies. Bobby Ross, who coached the San Diego Chargers in 1996, was hired to replace Wayne Fontes in Detroit. Dan Reeves, who has little love for Giants general manager George Young, was selected by Atlanta Falcons ownership to return to his native Georgia and resurrect an abysmal team. In New Orleans, Mike Ditka replaced the fired Jim Mora as the Saints' savior. Ditka's hiring had as much to do with selling tickets as it did with winning ballgames.

Lewis has Super Bowl rings to show for the impeccable job he has done as a member of both the San Francisco 49ers and Green Bay Packers coaching staffs. Mike Holmgren—who before being named Green Bay's coach in 1991 was the offensive coordinator for the 49ers—brought the cerebral Lewis with him from San Francisco to be the Packers' offensive coordinator.

---

1. As of 2004, there were several black coaches in the NFL, including Dennis Green, Tony Dungy, Lovey Smith, and Herman Edwards.

The Superior Performance of Black NFL Coaches

Average Wins per Full Season for Coaches, by Race and Stage of Career, 1986–2001

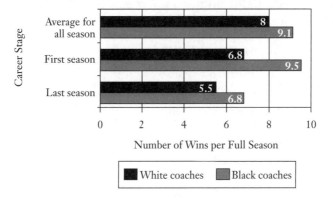

Johnnie L. Cochran Jr. and Cyrus Mehri, *Black Coaches in the National Football League: Superior Performance, Inferior Opportunities.* www.findjustice.com, September 30, 2002.

A Matter of Utmost Importance

San Francisco didn't even have the professional courtesy or decency to wait until after the Super Bowl (it is considered tampering to speak with a coach or even hint at an interest in his services while his team is still playing) to interview Lewis for their opening after parting ways with former coach George Seifert. Instead they plugged the hole with University of California coach Steve Mariucci, another former 49ers assistant who ironically worked under Lewis during his tenure there.

The worst example of Black coaches being ignored in favor of their white counterparts was the hiring of Dick Vermeil to change the fortunes of the St. Louis Rams. Out of football for the better part of two decades, Vermeil, who in his last NFL tour was coach of the Eagles, was working as an analyst for ABC primarily covering college football. He had no business being afforded the chance to become a head coach in the NFL once again before Lewis or Thomas were given their initial opportunity. It is wrong and league executives cannot just sit back and turn a blind eye.

To date, no official statement has been released by the NFL explaining their position on the subject. But this is an issue that they should not be allowed to trivialize and the matter should be of utmost importance to everyone affiliated with professional football.

The "It's My Bat and Ball" Syndrome

How, in 1997, almost 80 years since the great Fritz Pollard became the first African American to coach a professional football team (Pollard co-coached the Akron Pros to an 8-0-3 finish and the unofficial championship of the American Professional Football Association) has such overt inequity and biasness flourished?

"The 'It's my bat and ball' syndrome persists," said one Black assistant coach. "The owners figure they are in control so therefore they play by their own rules. Unfortunately, we are left on the outside looking in."

Attempts to reach Tagliabue were unsuccessful, as well as the three current Black head coaches and several assistants. When one assistant was contacted his response was: "Do you think I'm going to sit here and address this topic? I'm going to let you writers handle that. It's nothing but negatives. I'm not even going to grace that platform," he said with obvious anger and disappointment resonating with every word.

Giving Voice to Racism

What can be done to alter this pattern of racism? Black coaching candidates are reluctant to speak out for fear that what little chance they have of landing a head coaching position would be jeopardized. Some may view that approach as selling out or succumbing to the white power structure, which is the furthest assessment from the truth. These proud men have dedicated a lifetime to the sport and would certainly be labeled big mouths, trouble makers and rebellious, and subsequently would never be given a shot.

The established Black veteran players who are well respected around the league must become a powerful voice. The Reggie Whites and Emmitt Smiths and Jerry Rices must make their presence felt. Many of the current players have post-playing aspirations of becoming coaches. If today's athletes do not strongly state their feelings on the lack of opportunities being presented to coaches of color, they will find that doors will be slammed in their faces when they go knocking. A collaborative pioneering effort needs to be put in place immediately.

Journalists both Black and white must fess up to the truth and start exploring the topic more passionately. It is no secret that the media plays a major role in the firing and hiring of coaches. If Blacks are smart enough to play the game, then they sure as hell have the intelligence to be solid field generals. Pressure must be applied on the owners to reverse this disturbing practice.

For the moment, though, it seems as these millionaire, and in some instances billionaire, owners have little intentions of doing the right thing. And the myriad Black assistants can only sit back and watch as the color of their skin is the only reason they are being denied a fair opportunity.

| "Teams are simply not going to bypass promising black coaches who could help them win, just because of their race."

Minority Coaches Do Not Face Discrimination in Hiring

Part I: Roger Clegg; Part II: Greg Franke

Roger Clegg is general counsel for the Center for Equal Opportunity in Sterling, Virginia, an organization that opposes affirmative action and other polices involving racial preferences. In the first part of the following two-part viewpoint, Clegg takes issue with a 2002 report authored by lawyers Johnnie L. Cochran Jr. and Cyrus Mehri, which argued that black coaches face discrimination in hiring in the National Football League. Clegg maintains that statistics cited in the report are not evidence of discrimination. He also contends that the hiring practices suggested by Cochran and Mehri amount to a quota system. In the second part of the viewpoint, Greg Franke, a freelance writer, criticizes the NFL policy, adopted in the wake of the Cochran/Mehri report, that requires teams to interview at least one minority candidate when hiring coaches. Franke argues that the policy could lead to discrimination against better-qualified candidates.

As you read, consider the following questions:

1. Why does Clegg find the evidence of discrimination offered in the Cochran/Mehri report "doubtful"?
2. What coach does Franke believe is a victim of reverse discrimination?

I

Johnnie Cochran . . . and class-action lawyer Cyrus Mehri released [in September 2002] a report titled *Black Coaches in the National Football League: Superior Performance, Inferior Opportunities.* Can a lawsuit be far behind?

The report, available at www.findjustice.com, relies on a study prepared by Janice Madden, a "Professor of Sociology, Real Estate, and Regional Science" at the University of Pennsylvania, where she is also "Director of the Alice Paul Research Center and the Women's Studies program." Dr. Madden looks at the won-lost percentage of black coaches and concludes that they compare favorably to those of white coaches. Specifically, black coaches overall average 1.1 more wins per 16-game season, and win an average of 2.7 more games in their first season (9.5 versus 6.8), and 1.3 more games per season in the years they're fired. In addition, to test the argument that black coaches have simply been hired by better teams, Dr. Madden compared the won-lost records of whites and blacks within the same teams, and found that for these six teams the black coaches "had more wins than the white coaches who preceded them, and more than those who came after."

The report prompts four observations.

Questionable Conclusions

First, it is interesting that the better-than-average performance of black coaches is taken to be bad news. One might have thought that the data are encouraging, inasmuch as they provide evidence that black coaches are given the support they need by the front-office, the fans, and—most importantly—the players to do their job successfully. Indeed, had Dr. Madden's study come out the other way, one would not have been surprised had Cochran and Mehri adduced discrimination from that—the black coaches are so hamstrung by racism that they (literally) can't win.

Second, as for the claim that these numbers prove discrimination, that's very doubtful. Dr. Madden puts this footnote into her study:

The small number of black coaches hired by NFL teams

makes it difficult to conduct more formal statistical analyses of racial differences. While many of the racial differences reported here are strong enough that a 'statistical test dismisses chance or random variation as the reason for racial differences, in the end, there are simply too few black coaches for more formal statistical analyses to be appropriate.

Why, after all, would an owner want to hire anyone but the best qualified coach—that is, the coach who he thinks will win the most games? Owners want to make money and draw fans and have a successful play-toy—and all of that means that the team must win. It seems very unlikely that owners would be willing to forego all that simply to indulge their taste for racial discrimination.

Third, it is encouraging to see a willingness by these civil-rights lawyers to let objective performance criteria be the standard by which people ought to be selected and evaluated. Notice that, for once, there is no insistence that the focus be on whether the players are supplied with appropriate role models, for instance, or whether the fans' self-esteem is increased. The coach wins games or he doesn't, and that's what matters. Fair enough. We'll bear this in mind the next time someone complains that hiring on the merits has an illegal "disparate impact" on the basis of race.

Raising Awareness

The fourth and final point is the most important. Let's suppose, for the sake of argument, that there really is evidence that owners are discriminating against African Americans when it comes to hiring and firing coaches. If the discrimination is open-eyed and deliberate—that is, if the owners know that they aren't making rational decisions but they don't care because they are so bigoted—then it's not clear that anything can be done about it. But, as we've discussed, this seems very unlikely, since it will cost the owner fans, fame, and fortune.

So it must be that the discrimination is unconscious—that the owner doesn't realize that he's employing a double standard, but he is doing so nonetheless, to his own detriment. Well, if that's the case, then the report has done a valuable service, since the owners now know that they have to be on guard about some very bad decision-making that is costing them dearly.

Except, of course, that the report can't leave it at that. No, what the report suggests as a remedy is that the NFL adopt a "Fair Competition Resolution," which Cochran and Mehri have obligingly drafted. Indeed, the first item presented to those visiting the report on the law firm's website is a solicitation to send, via the law firm, this e-mail to NFL Commissioner Paul Tagliabue: "I am concerned about the low number of African-American headcoaches in the NFL and believe the NFL Commissioner and Team Owners must take action to promote fair competition." The law firm also requests, in the report itself, to be sent copies of any snail-mail letters to the commissioner. Perhaps the firm is preparing a list of disgruntled fans for a class-action lawsuit against the NFL.

Hiring Quotas Are Unfair

And what is the Fair Competition Resolution? A quota, of course, enforced by taking draft picks away from those teams that won't cooperate.

The problem, according to the resolution, is not discrimination, but "the lack of racial diversity"—something very different. Teams that diversify front office positions "through the hiring of qualified minority and female [where did they come from?] candidates" can be awarded additional draft picks. The idea, according to the report, is that "Diversity among key decision-makers will, over time, bring greater equity to the head coaching ranks." Even assuming that this is true, diversity—as opposed to nondiscrimination—is not worth the price of front-office hiring quotas.

But there's more. According to the resolution, teams must "compile and select from a racially diverse final candidate slate when hiring a Head Coach, Assistant Head Coach or Coordinator [again, there's no evidence in the report of discrimination regarding the latter two]." And if you're not willing to meet your quotas in compiling this slate, then, "For Head Coach positions, the Team shall forfeit a first round draft pick. For Assistant Coach and Coordinator positions, the Team shall forfeit a third round draft pick."

Cochran and Mehri will argue that this does not require anyone to be hired because of race. Rather, it just ensures that there is always a nonwhite among the finalists. But there are two responses to this.

For starters, it means that sometimes a better-qualified white candidate, and one who might have gotten the job, is going to be bumped off the list to make way for a less qualified nonwhite candidate. More direly, it is very unlikely that Cochran, Mehri, and other lawyers are going to be satisfied with a mere diverse slate. If the nonwhite is not hired, you can bet that he will demand to know why not, and they will make life very unpleasant for the owner. And, of course, the lawyers will know who the client will be in the forthcoming lawsuit.

II

In the frenzy over Rush Limbaugh's comments on ESPN, it's easy to overlook one very significant thing.[1] It just took a lightning-rod like Limbaugh to ignite it. Indeed, the episode was merely a symptom of an underlying cause.

To put things in perspective: Not long ago, before the plague of political correctness engulfed our society. professional sports (unlike collegiate sports, which has been ravaged by the egregious interpretation of Title IX) stood out as perhaps a final bastion of sanity.

For all its well-documented faults, big-league sports epitomized a wonderful American ideal: that anyone—regardless of race, creed, wealth, upbringing, or zodiac sign—can make it to the top. Just be among the best performers. Period. End of story.

Unfortunately, in perhaps a dress rehearsal for the Limbaugh affair, this ideal has come under assault.

The tipping point occurred [in July 2003] when the Detroit Lions were fined $200,000 for violating the league's new policy of requiring at least one minority candidate to be interviewed for any head coaching opening—even when a high-profile individual is already being sought. Almost everyone knows that in such a circumstance, minority "candi-

---

1. In September 2003 the conservative pundit argued that the media had been reluctant to criticize the play of NFL quarterback Donovan McNabb because he is black.

dates" would likely be nothing more than pawns in a ridiculous charade of putting race ahead of merit.

Unfortunately (as is disturbingly the case in our bureaucratic and litigious society), the views of sensible people don't count, if a few administrators, judges, or high-powered attorneys disagree.

The Lions (clearly intent on hiring Steve Mariucci) tried to comply, inviting five minorities for interviews, who—to their immense credit—wanted nothing to do with such a farce.

Lions president Matt Millen then did what any reasonable person would do—he hired Mariucci, who may well lead the Lions back to respectability.

Preferential Hiring Practices

Unfortunately, the NFL (nearly pulling a muscle performing the mental contortions necessary to arrive at such a decision) called an 'unnecessary common sense' penalty.

The league self-righteously lectured the Lions that, "While certain of the difficulties that you encountered in seeking to schedule minority candidates were beyond your control, you did not take sufficient steps to satisfy the commitment that you had made."

To add to the absurdity (if that's possible), teams were informed that future such "infractions" could bring a fine of $500,000 or more, while attorneys Cyrus Mehri and Johnnie Cochran demanded that teams even lose first-round draft choices!

The obvious question was: why were the steps taken by the Lions considered insufficient?

Don't expect an answer from the NFL.

In response to queries on the subject, the league's Vice President of Public Relations (the term 'public relations' is here applied loosely), Greg Aiello pointedly refused to make any comment, simply referring again and again to the league's nearly year-old press release that raises more questions than it answers.

So (especially in light of the latest fracas involving Rush Limbaugh) here's another question the NFL ought to consider—even if it won't share its deliberations with the public: Is it about to be destroyed by racial politics?

It certainly appears that league officials know very well that they have adopted an irrational policy regarding race.

But one should perhaps not be too hard on them.

After all, the NFL has been under intense legal and political pressure from the pseudo civil-rights crowd that insists on dividing people based on race, rather than recognizing the great progress that has been made over the past 40 years in race relations.

Consider that in Major League baseball in the late 1960s, among the primary reasons for the American League's decline was its dearth of black players.

In response, formerly recalcitrant teams began signing black players in droves, and within 10 years, the American League was again competitive with—or even superior to—the National League.

Treat Coaches as Individuals

[In 2004] Dick Vermeil, head coach of the Kansas City Chiefs, will likely retire. Therefore, as Randy Covitz noted in the *Kansas City Star*, the team "could be in the crosshairs of the minority-hiring issue and a target of [attorney Johnnie] Cochran's." What if, for example, the club "promotes assistant head coach Al Saunders and gives the impression it did not fairly consider minority candidates"? We are now into impressions. Perhaps the brave new social engineers should stop pussyfootin' around with this interviewing stuff and simply mandate the hiring of black head coaches—a certain percentage of the slots in the league. Say, half. Such a scenario is not altogether unthinkable, and it would have the benefit of cutting to the chase.

As always, things are infinitely easier when you judge people as people, and not as representatives of a race.

Jay Nordlinger, "Color in Coaching," *National Review*, September 1, 2003.

In the mid-seventies NFL, when the Pittsburgh Steelers inserted a black quarterback named Joe Gilliam, many foolishly believed that a black man was somehow incapable of playing that position. Now, nearly 30 years later, there have been numerous black quarterbacks who do not need media hype to be considered successful. (This, incidentally, would have been an intelligent response for those who disagreed with Limbaugh, instead of trying to suppress his viewpoint.)

The same process is occurring with black coaches, of whom there have already been several successful ones. Struggling NFL teams are simply not going to bypass promising black coaches who could help them win, just because of their race. And if any teams are that dumb, they'll be the losers when other teams snap up the talent that the intransigent ones could have had. Before long, all will emerge from the Dark Ages, just as has always happened before.

Furthermore, the NFL is doing much to encourage black advancement.

For example, it has an extensive program (the summer Minority Coaching Fellowship) that provides the opportunity for legions of prospective black coaches—81 this year alone—to gain invaluable experience that will undoubtedly lead to coaching positions for many of them. Unfortunately, such efforts seem not to register with the hyper-activists.

Of course, the problem with this kind of program is the 'whites need not apply' mentality that still discriminates by skin color.

Rejecting Qualified Candidates

One such victim of this misguided approach is Rick Denstorff, a 13-year college coaching veteran who has served as a graduate assistant, defensive line coach, and offensive co-ordinator at several different schools.

Having been repeatedly told that he could not be considered for subsequent college openings because the school in question had to hire a minority, he sought to get into an NFL camp as a volunteer coach, only to again hear the 'no whites allowed' refrain.

"The frustrating thing is when you see guys who have gotten positions right away over others who have better credentials, just because of race," Denstorff says. "And that goes both ways."

Ironically, NFL Commissioner Paul Tagliabue seems to agree, stating that "the principle of fair employment centers on the idea that employers should not hire less qualified or unqualified people while passing over members of minority groups who are more qualified."

Precisely—except that discrimination against any more qualified candidate is wrong, not just against minorities. But the commissioner didn't acknowledge that race extremists are not satisfied with mere equal opportunity. They want "equality of result," and will stop at nothing to get it, even if that means repudiating colorblind social policies.

Therefore, one can only imagine what will happen if the current policy does not result in more black coaches, and soon.

The obvious solution is to simply hire the best candidate available, regardless of race. But that novel concept seems too radical these days—in fact, any commentator who had the audacity to say that would probably have to resign under pressure, just like Rush Limbaugh!

Still, the NFL must realize that few will want to watch its games if the league is perceived as valuing political correctness over winning talent. Though understandably trying to protect itself from legal assault, at some point it will have to make a stand.

Maybe that will happen when the silent majority that opposes this nonsense finally revolts now that the race hustlers are messing with their football games!

"We are beginning to see the outcome of equal opportunity on the playing fields."

Title IX Is Necessary to Reduce Sexual Discrimination in Sports

Women's Sports Foundation

The Women's Sports Foundation (WSF) is a charitable educational organization dedicated to ensuring that girls and women have equal access to participation in sports. The following viewpoint is excerpted from a 2002 WSF report commenting on the thirtieth anniversary of Title IX of the Educational Amendments of 1972. Title IX bans sex discrimination in schools, whether it be in academics or athletics. WSF contends that Title IX has resulted in thousands more girls and young women participating in athletics. However, the WSF also maintains that women's high school and college sports are still funded at far lower levels than are men's sports, and that better enforcement of Title IX will help close this gap.

As you read, consider the following questions:

1. What is the percent increase of women participating in intercollegiate athletics in 2001 versus 1971, according to the authors?
2. How does WSF describe the record of Title IX enforcement from 1972 to 2002?
3. In the case of *Cohen v. Brown University*, why did a court reject the university's arguments, according to WSF?

For many, Title IX is synonymous with expanded opportunities in athletics. Its success is evidenced by women's and girls' increased participation in sports, the impressive achievements of the nation's female athletes, stunning advances in each summer and winter Olympic Games, and the creation of nationally televised professional women's basketball and soccer leagues over the last five years. It takes a large and vibrant base of general sports participants and 15 to 20 years of elite athlete support to create an Olympic gold medalist or professional athlete; years in which an athlete is given access to quality coaching, sports facilities, weight rooms, athletic scholarships and quality competition. Women and girls were virtually precluded from taking advantage of most athletic opportunities in schools before Title IX, but we are beginning to see the outcome of equal opportunity on the playing fields.

But Olympic medals and professional sports contracts are not what Title IX is all about. Rather, the quest for equal opportunity in sport has always been about the physiological, sociological and psychological benefits of sports and physical activity participation. Research studies commissioned by the Women's Sports Foundation in 1998 and 2000 found that girls who play sports enjoy greater physical and emotional health and are less likely to engage in a host of risky health behaviors (i.e., drug use, smoking, drinking) than non-participants. Other studies have linked sports participation to reduced incidences of breast cancer and osteoporosis later in life. Yet girls are twice as likely to be inactive as boys, and enjoy nearly 30% fewer opportunities to participate in both high school and college sports. Much distance remains between the current status of women and girls in sports and the ultimate goal of gender equity.

Participation Rates and Resource Allocation

Prior to 1972, women and girls looking for opportunities for athletic competition were more likely to become cheerleaders or secure places in the bleachers as spectators. In 1971, fewer than 295,000 girls participated in varsity athletics in American high schools, comprising a mere seven percent of all high school varsity athletes. The outlook for college women was equally grim: before Title IX, fewer than 30,000 females competed in intercollegiate athletics. Low participation rates reflected the lack of institutional commitment to providing athletics programming for women. Before Title IX, female college athletes received only two percent of overall athletic budgets. Athletic scholarships for women were effectively nonexistent.

Title IX's enactment has changed the playing field significantly. By 2001, nearly 2.8 million girls participated in athletics, representing 41.5 percent of varsity athletes in American high schools—more than an 847 percent increase from 1971. The progress on college campuses also has been impressive. Today, 150,916 women compete in intercollegiate sports, accounting for 43 percent of college varsity athletes—an increase of more than 403 percent from 1971. Contrary to media reports, men's participation levels at both the high school and college level have increased.

While significant, these gains still stop short of providing girls and women with their fair share of opportunities to compete. In the 1999–2000 year, female students represented approximately 54.2 percent of the student body at four-year colleges. Yet, only 23 percent of all NCAA [National Collegiate Athletic Association] Division I colleges provided athletic opportunities for women within five percentage points of female student enrollment. This percentage is up from nine percent for the 1995–1996 season.

Although the resources and benefits allocated to female athletes also have improved significantly since Title IX's passage, they still fall far short of what equity requires. After 30 years, the gap is still significant and closing much too slowly. Institutions are not exercising restraint on men's sports expenditures while women's sports catch up.

- In the past four years, for every new dollar going into athletics at the Division I and Division II level, male sports receive 58 cents while female sports receive 42 cents.
- Male athletes receive $133 million, or 36 percent more, than female athletes in college athletic scholarships each year at NCAA member institutions.
- On a per-athlete basis, colleges spent an average of

$2,983, $1,199 and $770 per female athlete in Divisions I, II and III, respectively, compared to the $3,786, $1,455 and $745 spent on male athletes.

National data on expenditures do not exist for girls' and boys' interscholastic sports, but anecdotal evidence suggests that similar financial disparities also exist at the elementary/secondary level.

Coaches, Administrators, and Other Athletic Personnel

Female coaches, athletic administrators, and women in other sports positions have not shared in the improved opportunities enjoyed by female students and athletes since Title IX's enactment. In the early 1970s, women head coaches led 90 percent of women's collegiate teams. By the 2001–2002 school year, female head coaches led only 44 percent of women's intercollegiate athletic teams, the lowest total since the passage of Title IX. This number is down from 47.7 percent in 1995–1996. Since 2000, 90 percent of the available head-coaching positions in women's athletics have gone to men. A similar decline in the percentage of women coaching girls' teams can be witnessed at the high school level.

To make matters worse, the loss of coaching opportunities in women's sports has not been offset by a corresponding increase in opportunities for women to coach men's teams. To the contrary, women are virtually shut out of these jobs, holding only two percent of the coaching positions in men's collegiate sports, a percentage that has remained constant over the last 30 years. Currently, there are no indications that the downward trend is slowing.

Women's college basketball, considered by most to be the greatest economic success among all women's collegiate sports, is one of few exceptions to diminishing coaching opportunities for women. The number of women intercollegiate basketball coaches has remained relatively constant over the past 10 years, with women currently holding 62.8 percent of these head coaching jobs. However, among 24 women's NCAA championship sports, female coaches are in the majority in only seven.

The impact of such sex discrimination on coaching opportunities for women is exacerbated by the striking disparity in the salaries paid to coaches of men's and women's teams. At the Division I level, men's basketball head coaches average $149,700. By contrast, women's basketball head coaches average $91,300 or 61 cents to the dollar paid to head coaches of men's basketball. This trend continues at the assistant coach level, where men's basketball assistant coaches average $44,000 while women's basketball assistant coaches average $34,000. Only in the sports of fencing, volleyball, and tennis, the sports paying the lowest salaries to coaches of male teams, do coaches of women's sports receive equal or greater pay than coaches of the equivalent male sports.

Athletic directors at the college level are also predominately male (83.1%). As the status and salary of such positions increase, female representation decreases (8.4% in Division I versus 25.5% in Division III). Males also dominate the positions of sports information director (87.7%) and athletic trainer (72.2%). As the competitiveness of a division and average salary increases, women's representation in these athletics positions also decreases. This trend remains true for every position except for head coaching jobs, for which gender representation in Division I and Division III is equal but average salaries are not.

Title IX Enforcement

The record of Title IX enforcement in interscholastic and intercollegiate athletics over the past 30 years is fair at best, as evidenced by the persistent disparities highlighted above. In 1975, the then Department of Health, Education and Welfare (HEW) issued federal Title IX regulations, which included sweeping requirements for equal athletic participation opportunities, proportional athletic scholarship funding, and equality in the treatment of and benefits provided to male and female athletes. The regulations allowed colleges and high schools a three-year phase-in period, and allowed elementary schools a one-year phase-in period. HEW explained the regulations in greater detail through a Policy Interpretation issued in 1979. However, enforcement in intercollegiate athletics was largely nonexistent throughout the 1980s, in part because of the Supreme Court's 1984 decision in *Grove City College v. Bell*. In *Grove City College*, the Court limited Title IX's application to the specific programs within colleges and universities that actually received federal funds (usually not the case for athletic programs), rather than applying Title IX to entire institutions should any of their programs receive federal funds. Congress overturned this decision in 1988 through the passage of the Civil Rights Restoration Act.

Female High School and Collegiate Sports Participation

Year	1971–1972	2000–2001	Percent Increase
High School Varsity Athletes			
Female	294,015	2,784,154	847 percent
Male	3,666,917	3,921,069	6.9 percent
Collegiate Varsity Athletes (NCAA)			
Female	29,977	150,916	403 percent
Male	170,384	208,866	23 percent

Women's Sports Foundation, *Title IX at 30: Athletes Receive C+*, June 13, 2002.

Even with the full scope of Title IX restored, little or no Title IX enforcement by The Office for Civil Rights (OCR) occurred. When colleges responded to budget constraints by cutting already beleaguered women's teams, parents and female athletes responded by taking their Title IX complaints to court. Numerous lawsuits in the 1990s resulted in the creation of a uniform body of law protecting the right to equal athletic opportunity regardless of sex, despite strenuous objections by defendants that men purportedly are more interested in playing sports than women, and therefore deserve disproportionate participation opportunities. Progress has been made largely on a case-by-case basis, with gains gradual and piecemeal. Most notably, in the case of *Cohen v. Brown University*, the First Circuit rejected the university's argument that women are less interested than men in playing sports because it rests on stereotypical notions about women and only perpetuates the discrimination that women face in athletics.

Other cases have helped root out discrimination by athletic associations, which control the athletic programs of colleges or high schools but claim that they have no responsibilities to comply with the civil rights laws. The Supreme Court decided otherwise in *Brentwood Academy v. Tennessee Secondary School Athletic Association*. The Court held that the high school athletic association is subject to the United States Constitution, which governs the conduct of government entities only, because the association is essentially an arm of the state. In *National Collegiate Athletic Association v. Smith*, the Supreme Court held that the NCAA is not subject to Title IX just because it receives dues from its federally funded member schools, but the Court specifically left open other legal arguments for coverage of athletic associations. One of these arguments was adopted by the court in *Communities for Equity v. Michigan High School Athletic Association*, in which a federal district court in Michigan held that the association is subject to Title IX, the Constitution, and Michigan state law. Accordingly, the court found that the association discriminated against girls by scheduling six girls' sports, but no boys' sports, in nontraditional or disadvantageous seasons.

The Backlash Against Title IX

Moreover, women's progress, albeit limited, has sparked a backlash by Title IX opponents who claim that Title IX has gone "too far" and has "hurt" men's sports. After holding hearings on this issue in May 1995, some Members of Congress asked OCR to revisit its 1979 Policy Interpretation and consider whether it should weaken its enforcement standards, particularly the equal participation requirement. In response, OCR strongly affirmed its longstanding interpretation through a 1996 Policy Clarification, which explains how institutions can and must comply with the equal participation opportunities requirement. Courts have also rejected suits brought by male athletes claiming their schools have discriminated against them by cutting or capping men's teams, holding that Title IX does not require these actions but gives schools flexibility in structuring their athletics programs as long as they treat men and women equally. Nonetheless, the challenges continue. In January 2002, the National Wrestling Coaches Association and other Title IX opponents filed a federal lawsuit against the U.S. Department of Education challenging the Title IX regulations and policy guidance regarding athletics opportunities; the government's response will indicate whether it will vigorously defend the longstanding athletics policies. [A federal court dismissed the lawsuit in June 2003.]

However, given the absence of equal opportunity after 30 years, OCR is not providing adequate leadership in enforcement efforts. In 2001, OCR initiated only two Title IX athletics reviews of institutions. This lack of enforcement by OCR, coupled with an increase in Title IX lawsuits, suggests that OCR's lack of enforcement has required aggrieved parties to seek relief through the court system. Parties filing lawsuits incur considerable costs and risk retribution. In light of the numbers of schools still not in compliance, OCR needs to step up its enforcement activities. Yet during the 30 years since Title IX's inception, not one institution has had its federal funding withdrawn because it is in violation of Title IX.

Recommendations:

- Congress should mandate data collection on the participation of high school students in physical education and high school athletics programs as part of the administration's proposal for the reauthorization of the Office for Educational Research and Improvement (OERI);
- The U.S. Department of Education should support the continuation of existing strong compliance standards and increase OCR enforcement of these standards;
- To encourage the filing of actionable complaints, OCR should develop a standard complaint form with a checklist of alleged Title IX violations;
- School athletic administrations should utilize the EEOC [Equal Employment Opportunity Commission] guidelines to make sure that they treat coaches of male and female sports equally. To find these guidelines, go to http://www.eeoc.gov/regs/index.html.

"[To comply with Title IX, many colleges] boost the number of [their] women athletes artificially by subtracting from the men's side of the sports ledger."

Title IX Has Harmed Men's Sports

Jessica Gavora

Jessica Gavora is the author of *Tilting the Playing Field: School, Sports, Sex, and Title IX*. In the following viewpoint she argues that Title IX has resulted in many colleges cutting men's sports programs. The original purpose of Title IX, in Gavora's view, was to ensure that men and women have equal opportunities to participate in school sports, but, through misguided court rulings and the efforts of feminist organizations, Title IX is now interpreted to mean that colleges must have the same percentage of female atheletes as there are women in the student body. Gavora describes the experiences of Providence College and James Madison University: Many women participate in sports at these institutions, writes Gavora, but to comply with Title IX's vision of gender equity, these schools had to cut men's sports programs.

As you read, consider the following questions:

1. Why did feminist groups push hard for the passage of the Equity in Athletics Disclosure Act, in Gavora's opinion?
2. What sports did Providence College eliminate to achieve compliance with Title IX, according to the author?
3. What is Women's Sports Foundation leader Donna Lopiano's strategy for achieving gender equity, as described by Gavora?

Jessica Gavora, "A Field of Nightmares: A Number of Male Sports Have Been Kicked Off Campus," *Women's Quarterly*, Spring 2002, p. 9. Copyright © 2002 by the Independent Women's Forum. Reproduced by permission.

Mike Scott came to Providence College in Rhode Island for one reason: to play baseball. His dad had played college ball, spent some time in the minors, and was now a high school baseball coach. The younger Scott had been playing baseball since he was old enough to hold a bat. Now he had his eye on a chance at the big time: to play in the majors.

Providence, Scott thought, was the place to begin his journey. Since joining the program as an assistant coach in 1991, head coach Charlie Hickey had worked to build the eighty-year-old Friars program into a northeast powerhouse. In the 1990s, the team began to attract NCAA [National Collegiate Athletic Association] tournament bids and recorded just one losing season.

A standout high school hitter, Scott briefly considered the baseball program at the University of New Hampshire. But when UNH announced that it was cutting baseball in order to comply with Title IX, a federal statute that has caused gender quotas in sports, he turned to Providence College. And although Coach Hickey couldn't offer him a scholarship, a spot on the team and a chance to play were enough. One crisp fall day in October 1998, just two weeks into the preseason practice schedule, Coach Hickey was summoned from the practice field into Providence athletic director John Marinatto's office. A few minutes later, he returned to the practice diamond with shocking news: The 1998–99 baseball season would be the Friars' last.

The reason was Title IX. Because Providence—like virtually every college and university—receives some federal money in some form, the school was legally bound to comply with the provisions of the law.

But Scott and his teammates were confused: What women had faced discrimination at Providence? The Catholic university had a strong program of athletics for females. Of the twenty varsity programs carried by the college, half were for women. No female athlete had filed a complaint of discrimination at Providence, and no investigation had found a pattern of discrimination that somehow had escaped a complaint. What, Scott and his teammates wondered, was wrong at Providence College?

The answer could be found in a set of statistics that Marinatto had compiled that fall and submitted to the Department of Education in Washington, D.C. The Equity in Athletics Disclosure Act (EADA) requires that all colleges and universities submit a mind-boggling array of detailed information on their sports programs, broken down by sex. Schools report the number of athletic participants by sex, the assignment of head coaches by sex, operating expenses by sex, recruitment expenses by sex, coaches' salaries by sex, and on and on. In addition, the EADA demands one statistic that has nothing to do with athletics: Schools must compile and submit the number of full-time undergraduates, by sex.

Feminist women's groups like the American Association of University Women (AAUW) pushed hard for passage of EADA—with data on the gender balance of the student body included—in order to expedite the process of bringing lawsuits against schools under Title IX. By framing the issue in terms of "equity" they were able to convince Congress to impose yet another bookkeeping burden on colleges and universities and create a taxpayer-funded database with which to pursue Title IX "proportionality." Previously, finding the data needed to bring a lawsuit under Title IX necessitated a little digging; but the EADA created a readymade client shopping list for trial lawyers. One glance at a school's EADA submission shows a would-be plaintiff's attorney whether a school is vulnerable to a Title IX lawsuit.

When Providence College filled out its EADA form in the fall of 1998, the findings sent shockwaves through the administration. Like the majority of colleges and universities today, Providence's student body was majority female, and growing more so, but its athletic program failed to keep pace. Drawn by the security of Providence's Catholic tradition, women comprised a whopping 59 percent of all students in the fall of 1998. Female student-athletes, however, were only 48 percent of all varsity athletes. This was well above the national average of 40 percent female athletic participation, but not enough to pass the Title IX "proportionality" test. Providence had "too many" male athletes—11 percent too many, to be exact. Adding enough women's teams to meet proportionality, Providence's Gender Equity

Compliance Committee calculated, would cost $3 million, a prohibitive expense for the school. Something had to give.

Cutting Men's Sports to Fulfill Quota Requirements

Seven years earlier, Providence's cross-town rival, Brown University, was sued by a group of female athletes when it attempted to de-fund two men's and two women's varsity teams in a cost-saving effort. The female athletes at Brown argued that cutting women's teams was illegal under Title IX because the university had not yet achieved proportionality—despite offering more teams for women than any other school in the country except Harvard. Brown decided to fight the lawsuit, arguing that Title IX required it to provide women equal opportunity to participate in athletics, not guarantee that they actually participate at the same rate as men. A series of adverse rulings led Brown all the way to the Supreme Court, which declined to hear the case. The result was that the rulings of the lower courts stood: Title IX was interpreted to mean that the university did, in fact, have an obligation to see that women participated in sports as enthusiastically as men. The case was a landmark in the institutionalization of quotas under Title IX. Colleges and universities across the country began to cut men's teams to comply with what the court had decreed was the correct interpretation of the law.

Thus, Providence College did what all colleges and universities are today increasingly forced to do: consult its lawyers. Their advice was direct: The only way for Providence to insulate itself from a Title IX lawsuit or federal investigation was somehow to add enough female athletes, or subtract enough male athletes, to close the gap. So instead of imposing double-digit tuition increases to raise the funds for new women's teams, Providence chose to boost the number of its women athletes artificially by subtracting from the men's side of the sports ledger.

"They were looking for three things," says Coach Hickey. "They were looking for which sports had the number of participants to cut to bring them closer to proportionality, which sports had the scholarships they could transfer to the women's side, and which sports had the operating budget they could save money on."

Providence baseball had it all: twenty-eight bodies on the

The Rise of Title IX Lawsuits

Title IX . . . says nothing about quotas based on population proportions. In fact, the law's creators emphatically argued against such things. "The thrust of the amendment is to do away with every quota," explained its chief Senate sponsor, Birch Bayh (D-Ind.). House sponsor Albert Quie (R-Minn.) similarly underscored that Title IX "would provide that there shall be no quotas in the sex anti-discrimination title."

Despite such intentions, Title IX has become, in the approving words of Rep. Maxine Waters (D.-Calif.), "the biggest quota you've ever seen.". . .

What happened? In 1979, following standard operating procedure, the federal Department of Health, Education, and Welfare issued a policy interpretation for athletics. Schools would be in compliance with Title IX, HEW decreed, if they met any one prong of a three-prong test: They could provide sporting opportunities to the sexes in numbers substantially proportionate to their respective enrollments"; they could show a "history of continuing program expansion"; or they could show they were already meeting the "interests and abilities" of women.

In the 1990s, federal courts elevated this interpretation to the level of law. At the same time, they focused on the proportionality test as the only definitive means to prove compliance. A 1992 court decision further established that plaintiffs could collect attorney's fees and damages, which substantially raised the stakes for colleges and universities. Once compensatory and punitive damages could be awarded in Title IX cases, the lawsuits effectively became self-financing. Even when damages aren't awarded, public interest attorneys can bill the court at several times their actual costs. In fact, enterprising lawyers don't even need aggrieved plaintiffs; suits can be filed by anyone based on aggregate numerical disparities. . . .

In short, what happened to Title IX is a classic Washington story. Ideological activists take words that appeal to a general sense of fair play, such as opportunity, and then redefine them. While they argue for their new definition in court, they simultaneously justify their actions to the public based on the old, common-sense understanding.

Michael W. Lynch, "Title IX's Pyrrhic Victory," *Reason*, April 2001.

playing field, seven scholarships split among them, and $380,000 in operating expenses. Coach Hickey implored the Providence administration to save baseball by allowing the program to raise the necessary funds itself. He was informed that if such a dispensation were granted, Providence baseball would also have to raise enough money to cover the creation of one or more womens teams necessary to compensate for retaining twenty-eight male athletes. In the end, the feasible solution was to cut, not add. By eliminating baseball, men's golf, and men's tennis and capping the number of men who competed on the remaining eight men's programs, Providence achieved "proportionality." Without the addition of a single women's athletic opportunity, the percentage of female athletes rose from 47 percent to 57 percent.

Suddenly, a season that had begun so hopefully for Mike Scott and Charlie Hickey took on even more importance. Determined to go out with a bang, not a whimper, Scott and his teammates redoubled their efforts on the playing field. Second baseman Paul Costello recalled a line from *Major League*, a movie about a faltering group of professional baseball players: "There's only one thing left to do: Win the whole #$%&* thing!" The team adopted it as their unofficial motto.

And Providence baseball did indeed go on to win the whole thing. The 1998–99 season was the most successful in the school's history. Scott's team won forty-three games in the regular season and then four more to capture the Big East championship. With Mike Scott setting the pace, they led the nation in hits and were ranked twenty-first in the country. At the NCAA regional championship tournament in Tallahassee, the Friars took on Florida State, ranked second nationally, to conclude their season. "We played like there was literally no tomorrow," says Hickey. But in the end, it didn't matter. The Friars lost to Florida State in the regional championship, and Scott and his teammates decided to keep their uniforms.

"Gender Equity"

Feminists call the struggle for proportionality under Title IX the pursuit of "gender equity." The Women's Sports Foundation (WSF) is perhaps the strongest advocate of Title IX and "gender equity" in sports, having as its mission to "increase and enhance sports and fitness opportunities for all girls and women."

Founded by tennis player Billie Jean King in 1974 in the after-glow of her victory over Bobby Riggs in the "Battle of the Sexes," the WSF is the most powerful advocacy group for female athletes in the country. Like most women's groups, it has benefited from friendly press coverage. But unlike most women's groups, the WSF has made genuine heroes its public face: women like Mia Hamm, Julie Foudy, and Michelle Akers of the championship U.S. Women's World Cup soccer team; Kym Hampton and Rebecca Lobo of the Women's National Basketball Association (WNBA); two-time heptathlon winner Jackie Joyner-Kersee, sprinter Gail Devers, swimmer Summer Sanders, and gold-medal-winning gymnast Dominique Moceanu. This strategy of capitalizing on the popularity of female athletes has made the WSF a magnet for corporate giving. General Motors and Merrill Lynch are generous supporters. Representatives of Reebok, Mervyn's of California, and the Sporting Goods Manufacturers Association sit on its board of trustees. Their support allows the WSF to rake in additional contributions at a glittering gala each year in New York City and dole out more than $1 million a year in grants and scholarships to female athletes.

But behind the appealing image of strong female athleticism that is the group's public face, the Women's Sports Foundation pursues a relentlessly political agenda: to turn the grant of opportunity for women guaranteed under Title IX into a grant of preference. Under the leadership of its street-fighting executive director, Donna Lopiano, a former All-American softball player and the former womens athletic director at the University of Texas, the WSF has done more than any other group to convince colleges and universities that compliance with Title IX means manipulating the numbers of male and female athletes.

Lopiano, who calls those who disagree with her version of equity "dinosaurs," came to the WSF in 1992 fresh from Austin, where she was instrumental in fomenting a landmark Title IX lawsuit against her own university for its failure to achieve proportionality. Lopiano was the first to admit that Texas wasn't guilty of any bias against women, only a failing to give them the preferences she believes they deserve.

The Texas case was a landmark because up to that point, court victories won by female athletes to create Title IX quotas had been limited to mandating the reinstatement of teams that had been cut. The Lopiano-inspired Texas case, in contrast, demanded that women's teams be added to fill the gender quota. Thanks to revenues brought in by Longhorn football, Texas had a bigger women's athletic budget than any other two schools in its conference combined. Still, female athletic participation—the responsibility of the recently departed Lopiano—was stuck at around 23 percent in the early 1990s. So even though the administration was already in the process of adding two women's sports, it settled before the case got to court, agreeing to reach proportionality by the 1995–96 academic year. Additional women's teams were added while non-scholarship male athletes—who, by outnumbering female non-scholarship athletes eighty-one to one, accounted for much of Texas "Title IX gap"—were cut.

Lopiano brought the same passion for gender engineering to the Women's Sports Foundation. Her strategy, she told reporters in 1992, was to "break the bank," forcing schools to spend so much to meet the gender quota that what she regarded as the corrupt, male-dominated edifice of collegiate sports would fall entirely and be replaced by "gender equity." And if schools wouldn't spend on athletics, Lopiano made sure they spent on litigation.

Under Lopiano the WSF has worked tirelessly to cultivate future litigants and future complainants in Title IX cases. It maintains an equity hotline complete with a staff ready to assist attorney referrals, "how-to" literature, and expert assistance on everything from the rights of local girls' softball leagues to the arcana of federal regulations. There is an online database that ranks schools according to their commitment to gender equity and allows users to automatically share that ranking with local media and state and federal politicians. To keep Congress and the media aware of its efforts, the WSF sponsors National Girls and Women in Sports Day. Events are staged across the country and female athletes flood their congressmen's and senator's offices to remind them of the importance of gender equity in athletics.

But the Women's Sports Foundation, however formidable, is only one part of a coalition of liberal women's groups, trial lawyers, and "gender equity" advocates and consultants for whom Title IX is the sine qua non of existence. The American Association of University Women focuses on Title IX issues outside sports. And the National Women's Law Center (NWLC), another major player in the battle for gender equity in athletics, provides critical legal support.

Any attempt to change Title IX enforcement, even in a small way, will meet with great resistance from these groups. "The law means everything," says Donna de Varona, former Olympic swimming champ and WSF founding member. "Sports are the most visible affirmation of what Title IX did. But if you look behind it—if you look at the success of women in business, the success of women as lawyers, as leaders, and, hopefully, as politicians—our very lifeblood depends on Title IX."

James Madison University's "Title IX Gap"

At James Madison University, as at the majority of universities, women were a rising majority of the student body in 2000 but a lagging minority of athletes, even though JMU offered its women more athletic teams than most schools—and more than it offered its men. Lady Dukes ran track and cross-country, played basketball, volleyball, tennis, soccer, lacrosse, golf, and field hockey. They even shot archery, fenced, and swam. What they didn't do was engage in these team activities at the same rate as JMU men. The result was that in the 2000–01 school year, females were 58 percent of the James Madison student body but only 41 percent of student-athletes.

James Madison was failing [to achieve Title IX proportionality], and Al Taliaferro knew it. So on April 2, 2000, Taliaferro, the father of a senior on the JMU women's club softball team, wrote the Department of Education's Office for Civil Rights (OCR) to complain. Despite earlier assurances from university officials, Taliaferro wrote, JMU had not upgraded his daughter's softball team from partially funded club status to university-funded varsity status. Using JMU's Equity in

Athletics Disclosure form documenting JMU's seventeen-point "Title IX gap" as his resource, Taliaferro contended that the refusal to upgrade his daughter's team, given the disparity of participation in women's and men's athletics at JMU, was illegal under federal law. "James Madison has blatantly discriminated in violation of Title IX on the basis of sex against female athletes for many years," he wrote. The university, he demanded, must create a varsity softball team "immediately, without further delay." Either that, Taliaferro insisted, or "the college should be forced to eliminate its baseball program until it can provide equity to both programs."

James Madison officials [were forced] to take Taliaferro's remarks seriously. At minimum, his complaint would trigger a lengthy, expensive investigation by federal officials that was likely to come out badly for JMU. At maximum, the school could lose its federal funding. The officials wanted to do the right thing, but they couldn't afford to increase the size of their women's sports program. While other schools in their conference offered an average of eighteen teams, JMU featured a whopping twenty-seven. . . .

Administrators reached out to a "gender equity" consultant for guidance on what to do. The consultant, a veteran of two decades of service in the OCR, advised them that . . . as long as the university had failed to achieve proportionality, parents like Taliaferro could insist—and the federal government would agree—that JMU was out of compliance with the law. And as long as they were out of compliance with the law, they must add women's teams, whether or not they could afford to.

Harming Men, Not Helping Women

To resolve the complaint and shield itself from future lawsuits, James Madison saw no option other than to make wholesale cuts in its athletic program. Five men's teams and three women's teams were slated for elimination at the end of the 2000–01 academic year. Over a hundred athletes, many with years of eligibility left, would suddenly be downgraded from student-athlete to plain old student. The result was that fewer opportunities to play would be offered to everyone, but they would be offered in the right proportion: 58 percent for women and 42 percent for men—a mirror image of the student body. Opportunities for women wouldn't increase, and opportunities for men would definitely decline, by 107 team positions. But with the plan, James Madison officials felt safe from future Office for Civil Rights complaints or lawsuits.

In the end, under pressure from alumni and students, JMU decided to reach proportionality not by out-and-out killing the teams, just by taking away all their scholarship aid. Officials eliminated scholarships in eight men's teams and four women's teams, leaving four men's and nine women's teams that receive athletic aid. The legal issue was solved, but bad feelings lingered.

Stephen Reynolds, a senior on the men's gymnastic team, was one of those who lost his aid. It was his second Title IX athletics loss in four years. Reynolds had first attended Syracuse University; where his team was cut for the same reason. He came to JMU hoping to finish his education with his new teammates. "This was my team, these were the people I saw every single day, for three or four hours a day. I didn't want to see my teammates go through what we did at Syracuse," says Reynolds. "Title IX was never meant to do this."

Periodical Bibliography

The following articles have been selected to supplement the diverse views presented in this chapter.

Pamela Burdman	"Old Problem, New Solution? Can Programs Such as the NCAA's Leadership Institute for Ethnic Minority Males Boost the Numbers of Black Head Coaches, Athletic Directors?" *Black Issues in Higher Education*, April 11, 2002.
Ben Carrington and Ian McDonald	"Sports, Racism, and Inequality," *Sociology*, February 2002.
Steve Chapman	"Black QBs, QED: The End of an NFL Myth," *National Review*, September 17, 2001.
Ruth Conniff	"Title IX: Political Football," *Nation*, March 24, 2003.
Michael Eric Dyson	"Some Pain, Some Gain," *Sports Illustrated*, December 29, 2003.
Gerald Early	"Performance and Reality: Race, Sports, and the Modern World," *Nation*, August 10, 1998.
D. Stanley Eitzen and Maxine Baca Zinn	"The Dark Side of Sports Symbols," *USA Today Magazine*, January 2001.
Ben Hammer	"Reconsidering the Status of Title IX," *Black Issues in Higher Education*, April 10, 2003.
Nancy Hogshead-Makar	"The Ongoing Battle over Title IX," *USA Today Magazine*, July 2003.
Alan Hughes and Mark W. Wright	"Black Men Can't Coach?" *Black Enterprise*, July 2003.
Michael W. Lynch	"Title IX's Pyrrhic Victory," *Reason*, April 2001.
Kenan Malik	"Why Black Will Beat White at the Olympics," *New Statesman*, September 18, 2000.
John J. Miller	"What's in a (Team) Name?: The War Against Indian Symbols," *National Review*, April 16, 2001.
Michele Orecklin	"Now She's Got Game," *Time*, March 3, 2003.
S.L. Price	"Whatever Happened to the White Athlete?" *Sports Illustrated*, December 8, 1997.
Time	"Flat-Out Fantastic," July 19, 1999.

CHAPTER 4

Is Drug Use a Problem in Sports?

Chapter Preface

The principal argument against the use of performance-enhancing drugs in sports is that it is not fair. Opponents of "doping" in sports view it as a form of cheating, not unlike using a corked bat in baseball. The analogy shows that drugs are far from the only thing (besides practice and training) that can give an athlete a competitive edge. Amidst all the controversy over the use of steroids and other substances by athletes, some journalists have warned of a future in which drugs are only one of the ways in which people can artificially increase their athletic ability.

For example, in 2002 researchers at Johns Hopkins University were able to manipulate the genes in laboratory mice that affect muscle development, creating mice that were visibly bigger and stronger than normal. This prompted speculation about the sports applications of genetic engineering—or "gene doping," as some sportswriters have called it.

The still experimental process of gene therapy—the transfer of new genes into the bodies of patients—has for several years been hailed as a way to treat all manner of diseases. It could also potentially be used to improve athletic performance by stimulating an athlete's muscle growth, increasing the oxygen-carrying capacity of his or her blood, or through other inventive applications.

"If it does take off, sport as we know it will disappear," warns Dick Pound, president of the World Anti-Doping Agency, a body set up by the International Olympic Committee. Other writers are not so sure. In the *Atlantic Monthly*, bioethics professor Michael J. Sandel writes that "it has always been the case that some athletes are better endowed genetically than others, and yet we do not consider this to undermine the fairness of competitive sports."

Gene doping is still years, perhaps decades, away from becoming a reality. But the questions surrounding it—What is fair? How far should an athlete go to improve performance? —mirror the issues involved in the use of steroids and other performance-enhancing substances. In the following chapter authors debate both the prevalence and the ethics of drug use in sports.

"Steroid use . . . is now so rampant in baseball that even pitchers and wispy outfielders are juicing up."

Steroid Use in Major League Baseball Is Widespread

Tom Verducci

In the following viewpoint Tom Verducci, a reporter for *Sports Illustrated*, maintains that steroid use among Major League baseball players is more widespread than ever before. Players take steroids, according to the author, to increase their muscle mass in order to improve their ability to hit home runs or throw fast pitches. Some players, writes Verducci, also take growth hormones, and have unnatural facial characteristics as a result. The author argues that steroids help make average players into extraordinary hitters. He concludes that the problem of steroid use in baseball will likely not be addressed until someone is seriously injured or killed as a result of steroid use.

As you read, consider the following questions:

1. What percentage of pro baseball players did Jose Canseco estimate use steroids, according to Verducci?
2. For what is human growth hormone normally prescribed?
3. How might athletes circumvent a drug testing scheme, in the author's view?

Tom Verducci, "Totally Juiced," with reporting by Don Yaeger, George Dohrmann, Luis Fernando Llosa, and Lester Munson, *Sports Illustrated*, vol. 96, June 3, 2002, p. 34. Copyright © 2002 by Time, Inc. All rights reserved. Reproduced by permission.

Arizona Diamondbacks righthander Curt Schilling thinks twice before giving a teammate the traditional slap on the butt for a job well-done. "I'll pat guys on the ass, and they'll look at me and go, 'Don't hit me there, man. It hurts,'" Schilling says. "That's because that's where they shoot the steroid needles."

The Texas Rangers were packing their gear after the final game of a road series last year [2001] when a player accidentally knocked over a small carry bag by his locker. Several vials of steroids spilled out and rolled on the clubhouse carpet. The player, hardly embarrassed or concerned, gave a slight chuckle and scooped them up. No one else in the room showed any surprise.

Steroid use, which a decade ago was considered a taboo violated by a few renegade sluggers, is now so rampant in baseball that even pitchers and wispy outfielders are juicing up—and talking openly among themselves about it. According to players, trainers and executives interviewed by *Sports Illustrated* . . . , the game has become a pharmacological trade show. What emerges from dozens of interviews is a portrait of baseball's intensifying reliance on steroids and other performance-enhancing drugs. These drugs include not only human growth hormone (hGH) but also an array of legal and illegal stimulants, ranging from amphetamines to Ritalin to ephedrine-laced dietary supplements, that many big leaguers pop to get a jolt of pregame energy and sharpen their focus. But it is the use of illegal steroids that is growing fastest and having a profound impact on the game.

The surest sign that steroids are gaining acceptance in baseball: the first public admission of steroid use—without remorse—by a prominent former player. Ken Caminiti, whose 15-year big league career ended after a stint with the Atlanta Braves last season, revealed to *Sports Illustrated* that he won the 1996 National League Most Valuable Player award while on steroids he purchased from a pharmacy in Tijuana, Mexico. Spurred to try the drugs by concern over a shoulder injury in early '96, Caminiti said that his steroid use improved his performance noticeably and became more sophisticated over the next five seasons. He told *Sports Illustrated* that he used steroids so heavily in '96 that by the end of that season, his testicles shrank and retracted; doctors found that his body had virtually stopped producing its own testosterone and that his level of the hormone had fallen to 20% of normal. "It took four months to get my nuts to drop on their own," he said of the period after he stopped taking the drugs.

Yet Caminiti, a recovering alcoholic and former drug user, defended his use of steroids and said he would not discourage others from taking them because they have become a widely accepted—even necessary—choice for ballplayers looking for a competitive edge and financial security. "I've made a ton of mistakes," said Caminiti. "I don't think using steroids is one of them."

No Secret

"It's no secret what's going on in baseball. At least half the guys are using steroids. They talk about it. They joke about it with each other. The guys who want to protect themselves or their image by lying have that right. Me? I'm at the point in my career where I've done just about every bad thing you can do. I try to walk with my head up. I don't have to hold my tongue. I don't want to hurt teammates or friends. But I've got nothing to hide.

"If a young player were to ask me what to do," Caminiti continued, "I'm not going to tell him it's bad. Look at all the money in the game: You have a chance to set your family up, to get your daughter into a better school. . . . So I can't say, 'Don't do it,' not when the guy next to you is as big as a house and he's going to take your job and make the money."

Anabolic steroids elevate the body's testosterone level, increasing muscle mass without changes in diet or activity, though their effect is greatly enhanced in conjunction with proper nutrition and strength training. Steroids are illegal in the U.S. unless prescribed by a physician for medical conditions, such as AIDS and hypogonadism (an inability to produce enough testosterone). Studies have shown that the side effects from steroids can include heart and liver damage, persistent endocrine-system imbalance, elevated cholesterol levels, strokes, aggressive behavior and the dysfunction of genitalia. Doctors suspect that steroid use is a major factor in the recent increase in baseball injuries, especially severe injuries such as complete muscle tears.

Unlike the NFL and NBA, both of which ban and test for steroid use—the NHL does neither—Major League Baseball has no steroid policy or testing program for big leaguers. (Baseball does test minor league players, but violators are neither penalized nor required to undergo counseling.)[1] Any such program would have to be collectively bargained with the Major League Baseball Players Association, which traditionally has resisted any form of drug testing but now faces a division in its membership over this issue. "Part of our task is to let a consensus emerge," says Gene Orza, the associate general counsel for the players union.

"No one denies that it is a problem," says commissioner Bud Selig. "It's a problem we can and must deal with now, rather than years from now when the public says, 'Why didn't you do something about it?' I'm very worried about this."

Increasing Acceptance

But it is also true that fans have become more accepting of steroids as part of the game. [In 1988] the crowd at Fenway Park in Boston chided Oakland A's outfielder Jose Canseco during the American League Championship Series with damning chants of "Ster-oids! Ster-oids!" The game had never before seen a physical marvel such as Canseco, a 240-pound hulk who could slug a baseball 500 feet and still be swift enough to steal 40 bases. Upon retiring [in May 2002] after failing to catch on with a major league team, Canseco, while not admitting steroid use himself, said that steroids have "revolutionized" the game and that he would write a tell-all book blowing the lid off drug use in the majors. Canseco estimated that 85% of major leaguers use steroids.

Heavily muscled bodies like Canseco's have now become so common that they no longer invite scorn. Players even find dark humor in steroid use. One American League outfielder, for instance, was known to be taking a steroid typi-

1. Major League Baseball implemented a new drug testing program for its 2003 season. As with the minor league system, players who test positive receive treatment rather than suspension.

cally given by veterinarians to injured, ill or overworked horses and readily available in Latin America. An opposing player pointed to him and remarked, "He takes so much of that horse stuff that one day we're going to look out in the outfield and he's going to be grazing."

Steroids have helped build the greatest extended era of slugging the game has ever seen—and, not coincidentally, the highest rate of strikeouts in history. Power, the eye candy for the casual fan, is a common denominator among pitchers and hitters, as hurlers, too, juice up to boost the velocity of their pitches.

Schilling says that muscle-building drugs have transformed baseball into something of a freak show. "You sit there and look at some of these players and you know what's going on," he says. "Guys out there look like Mr. Potato Head, with a head and arms and six or seven body parts that just don't look right. They don't fit. I'm not sure how [steroid use] snuck in so quickly, but it's become a prominent thing very quietly. It's widely known in the game.

"We're playing in an environment in the last decade that's been tailored to produce offensive numbers anyway, with the smaller ballparks, the smaller strike zone and so forth," Schilling continues. "When you add in steroids and strength training, you're seeing records not just being broken but completely shattered.

"I know guys who use and don't admit it because they think it means they don't work hard. And I know plenty of guys now are mixing steroids with human growth hormone. Those guys are pretty obvious."

Human Growth Hormone

If steroids are the cement of body construction, then human growth hormone is the rebar, taken in an attempt to strengthen joints so they can hold the added muscle mass produced by steroids. Human growth hormone can be detected only in specific blood tests, not the standard urine test used for other performance-enhancing drugs. It is prescribed to treat dwarfism in children, but it can also change a mature person's body structure and facial characteristics. Players joke about the swollen heads, protruding brows and lantern jaws of hGH users. "And they talk like this," Caminiti says, pushing his tongue to the front of his mouth and stammering, "because the size of their head changes." One major league executive knows of a star player whose hat size has grown two sizes in his late 30s.

Says Chad Curtis, an outfielder who retired [in 2001] after 10 seasons with six clubs, including three (1997 to '99) with the Yankees, "When I was in New York, a player there told me that hGH was the next big thing, that that's the road the game's heading down next. Now you see guys whose facial features, jawbones and cheekbones change after they're 30. Do they think that happens naturally? You go, 'What happened to that guy?' Then you'll hear him say he worked out over the winter and put on 15 pounds of muscle. I'm sorry, working out is not going to change your facial features."

"Here's one easy way to tell," says a veteran American League infielder who asked not to be identified. He grabbed a batting helmet and put it on the top of his head without pushing it down for the proper fit. "They can't get their helmet to go all the way down. It sits up on their heads. You see it all the time. You see this new culture of young players coming in, caught up in the vanity of getting big. They're bloated and ripped, and they shave their chests [to accentuate their physiques]. It's gotten to the point where more guys use [steroids or hGH] than don't use."

The infielder says that [in 2001] he asked a star teammate, whom he suspected of steroid use, why he used. The star replied, "It's a personal decision. It's like taking aspirin. Some people choose to take it and some don't. I respect somebody's choice one way or the other."

Improved Performance

Clearly, the players who choose to use steroids do so because they believe the drugs work. "It's still a hand-eye coordination game, but the difference [with steroids] is the ball is going to go a little farther," Caminiti says. "Some of the balls that would go to the warning track will go out. That's the difference."

The improvement steroids have made in some players has been striking. Says one veteran National League general manager, "You might expect the B player to become an A player with steroids. But now you see the C player go to an A player. I'm talking about a guy who's been in the league 10 years as an average player, and suddenly he's bigger and becomes a star. That's very troublesome."

Another National League G.M. tells a story about an overweight, lumpy backup player who had kicked around the fringes of the major leagues. "We signed him, and two years later the guy looked like someone in a muscle magazine," he says. The player, by then in his 30s, won a starting job for the first time and, with a decent season, earned a multiyear contract. He subsequently suffered a series of muscle tears and ruptures and was quickly out of baseball. "He was gone that fast," the G.M. says. "But the contract probably set up him for life. Other guys see that."

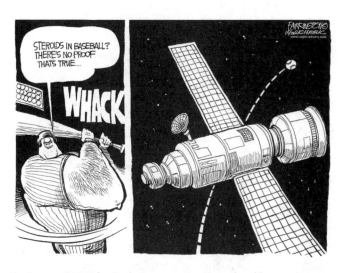

Farrington. © 2002 by Cagle Cartoons, Inc. Reproduced by permission.

Says Texas lefthander Kenny Rogers, "Basically, steroids can jump you a level or two. The average player can become a star, and the star player can become a superstar, and the superstar? Forget it. He can do things we've never seen before. You take a guy who already has great hand-eye coordination and make him stronger, and without a doubt he'll be better."

Steroids might even help a player become an MVP.

Caminiti was playing third base for the San Diego Padres in a series against the Houston Astros in April 1996 when Derrick May hit a flare into short leftfield. Caminiti dived for the ball, landed hard on his left elbow and shoulder, and tore his rotator cuff. "For the next six or seven days I couldn't lift my arm," he says. "I played for a month and a half in pure pain." Finally, he says, he decided to do something "to get me through the season." Caminiti had heard of players taking steroids to help them through injuries. He knew where to go.

"When you play in San Diego, it's easy to just drive into Mexico," he says.

Anabolic steroids are readily available in parts of Latin America as an over-the-counter item at farmacias that, in Mexican border towns such as Tijuana, cater to an American trade. Caminiti says he purchased a steroid labeled testosterona "to get me through the second half of the season." Then 33, he was playing in his 10th big league season. Never had he hit more than 26 home runs. He exceeded that in the second half alone, belting 28 homers after the All-Star break. He finished the year with 40 home runs, 130 RBIs (his previous best was 94) and a .326 batting average (24 points better than his previous high). He won the MVP award unanimously. . . .

Bigger Players

And steroids are not just for sluggers anymore. They're used by everyone, from erstwhile singles hitters to aging pitchers. Says Rogers, "Just look around. You've got guys in their late 30s, almost 40, who are throwing the ball 96 to 99, and they never threw that hard before in their lives. I'm sorry. That's not natural evolution. Steroids are changing the game. You've got players who say, 'All I want to do is hit,' and you have pitchers who say, 'All I want to do is throw 97. I don't care if I walk [everyone].'" Steroids have helped even mediocre pitchers turn up the heat. "The biggest change I've seen in the game," says a veteran major league infielder, "is seeing middle relievers come into the game throwing 91, 92 [mph]. Those guys used to be in the mid-80s or so. Now everybody is throwing gas, including the last guy in the bullpen."

The changes in the game are also evident in the increasingly hulking physiques of the players. The average weight of an All-Star in 1991 was 199 pounds. Last year it was 211. "We're kidding ourselves if we say this problem is not happening," says [San Diego Padres general manager Kevin] Towers. "Look at the before and after shots, at the size of some of these players from the '90s to now. It's a joke."

Barry Bonds of the San Francisco Giants is often cited as a player who dramatically altered his size and his game, growing from a lithe, 185-pound leadoff hitter into a 230-pound force who is one of the greatest home run hitters of all time. Bonds's most dramatic size gains have come in the past four years, over which he has doubled his home run rate. Bonds, who insists he added muscle through diet and intense training, has issued several denials of rumors that he uses steroids, including one to a group of reporters in April [2002] in which he said, "You can test me and solve that problem [of rumors] real quick."

But there is no testing in baseball, and everyone continues to speculate. What's a little speculation and innuendo these days anyway? Mark McGwire was cheered in every park on his march to 70 home runs in 1998 by fans hardly concerned about his reluctant admission that he'd used androstendione, an over-the-counter supplement that reputedly has the muscle-building effects of steroids.

"If you polled the fans," says former outfielder [Chad] Curtis, "I think they'd tell you, 'I don't care about illegal steroids. I'd rather see a guy hit the ball a mile or throw it 105 miles an hour.'"

Says Caminiti, "They come to the arena to watch gladiators. Do they want to see a bunch of guys choking up on the bat against pitchers throwing 82 miles an hour or do they want to see the ball go 500 feet? They want to see warriors.". . .

Baseball's Steroid Culture

The first generation of ballplayers who have grown up in the steroid culture is only now arriving, biceps bulging, chests shaven and buttocks tender. The acceptance level of steroids in the game may very well continue rising until . . . until what? A labor deal that includes a comprehensive testing plan? Such a plan, unlikely as it is, given the union's resistance, might deter some players, but even baseball officials concede that the minor league testing program in place gives players the green light to shoot up in the off-season. And athletes in other sports subject to testing have stayed one step ahead of enforcement with tactics such as using so-called "designer drugs," steroids that are chemically altered to mask the unique signature of that drug that otherwise would show on a urine test.

So even with testing, will it take something much darker for steroids to fall from favor? Renowned sports orthopedist James Andrews recalled the impact of two prominent deaths on the drug culture in football. "Major League Baseball can't continue to leave this door open," says Andrews. "Steroids became a big deal in football after Lyle Alzado [died] and ephedrine became a big deal after Korey Stringer. You don't want to see it get to that [in baseball] before someone says stop. But, unfortunately, that's what it seems to take to wake people up."

Rogers has a nightmare about how it might end, and that is why he does not always throw his fastball as hard as he can. It is the thought of some beast pumped up on steroids whacking a line drive off his head. "We're the closest ones to the hitter," he says of the men on the mound. "I don't want the ball coming back at me any faster. It's a wonder it hasn't happened already. When one of us is down there dead on the field, then something might happen. Maybe. And if it's me, I've already given very clear instructions to my wife: Sue every one of their asses. Because everybody in baseball knows what's been going on."

"Before [baseball] can solve its steroid problem, it must determine whether it even has one."

The Problem of Steroid Use in Major League Baseball Is Exaggerated

Dayn Perry

In the following viewpoint Dayn Perry, a freelance sportswriter, argues that the hysteria surrounding steroid use in professional baseball is unfounded. Perry maintains that the various estimates about how many Major Leaguers use steroids are baseless, and that even if many players are using steroids, there is little proof that it causes harm to the players or to baseball. He also suggests that steroid use cannot substitute for talent.

As you read, consider the following questions:

1. How many epidemiological studies about the long-term use of steroids have been conducted in the past sixty-five years, according to the author?
2. What new baseball stadiums does Perry believe have played a role in the home run surge of the 1990s?
3. How did Barry Bonds achieve his remarkable home run totals, according to Chris Yeager?

Dayn Perry, "Pumped Up Hysteria," *Reason*, vol. 64, January 2003, p. 32.

Had Ken Caminiti been a less famous ballplayer, or had he merely confessed his own sins, then it would have been a transient controversy. But it wasn't. Last May [2002], Caminiti, in a cathartic sit-down with Tom Verducci of *Sports Illustrated*, became the first major league baseball player, current or retired, to admit to using anabolic steroids during his playing days. Specifically, he said he used them during the 1996 season, when he was named the National League's Most Valuable Player. And his truth session didn't stop there.

"It's no secret what's going on in baseball. At least half the guys are using [steroids]," Caminiti told *SI*. "They talk about it. They joke about it with each other. . . . I don't want to hurt fellow teammates or fellow friends. But I've got nothing to hide."

The suggestion that steroids are a systemic problem in professional athletics is hardly shocking, but such candor from players—particularly baseball players, who until recently weren't subject to league-mandated drug testing—was virtually unheard of. Before the Caminiti flap had time to grow stale, Jose Canseco, another high-profile ex-ballplayer, upped the ante, declaring that a whopping 85 percent of current major league players were "juicing."

Dubious Accusations

The estimates were unfounded, the sources unreliable, and the implications unclear. But a media orgy had begun. The questions that are being asked of the players—Do you think it's worth it? How many are using? Why did the players union wait so long to adopt random testing? Why won't you take a test right now?—are mostly of the "Have you stopped beating your wife?" variety. The accusation is ensconced in the question.

This approach may be satisfying to the self-appointed guardians of baseball's virtue, but it leaves important questions unexplored. Indeed, before the sport can solve its steroid problem, it must determine whether it even has one.

From those sounding the clarion call for everything from stricter league policies to federal intervention, you'll hear the same two-pronged concern repeated time and again: Ballplayers are endangering their health and tarnishing baseball's competitive integrity. These are defensible, if dogmatic, positions, but the sporting media's fealty to them obscures the fact that both points are dubious.

A more objective survey of steroids' role in sports shows that their health risks, while real, have been grossly exaggerated; that the political response to steroids has been driven more by a moral panic over drug use than by the actual effects of the chemicals; and that the worst problems associated with steroids result from their black-market status rather than their inherent qualities. As for baseball's competitive integrity, steroids pose no greater threat than did other historically contingent "enhancements," ranging from batting helmets to the color line. It is possible, in fact, that many players who use steroids are not noticeably improving their performance as a result.

There are more than 600 different types of steroids, but it's testosterone, the male sex hormone, that's most relevant to athletics. Testosterone has an androgenic, or masculinizing, function and an anabolic, or tissue-building, function. It's the second set of effects that attracts athletes, who take testosterone to increase their muscle mass and strength and decrease their body fat. When testosterone is combined with a rigorous weight-training regimen, spectacular gains in size and power can result. The allure is obvious, but there are risks as well.

Health Effects

Anecdotal accounts of harrowing side effects are not hard to find—everything from "'roid rage" to sketchy rumors of a female East German swimmer forced to undergo a sex change operation because of the irreversible effects of excess testosterone. But there are problems with the research that undergirds many of these claims. The media give the impression that there's something inevitably Faustian about taking anabolics—that gains in the present will undoubtedly exact a price in the future. Christopher Caldwell, writing recently in the *Wall Street Journal*, proclaimed, "Doctors are unanimous that [anabolic steroids] increase the risk of heart disease, and of liver, kidney, prostate and testicular cancer."

This is false. "We know steroids can be used with a reasonable measure of safety," says Charles Yesalis, a Penn State epidemiologist, steroid researcher for more than 25 years, and author of the 1998 book *The Steroids Game*. "We know this because they're used in medicine all the time, just not to enhance body image or improve athletic performance." Yesalis notes that steroids were first used for medical purposes in the 1930s, some three decades before the current exacting standards of the Food and Drug Administration (FDA) were in place.

Even so, anabolic steroids or their derivatives are commonly used to treat breast cancer and androgen deficiencies and to promote red blood cell production. They are also used in emerging anti-aging therapies and to treat surgical or cancer patients with damaged muscle tissue.

Caldwell cites one of the most common fears: that anabolics cause liver cancer. There is dubious evidence linking oral anabolics to liver tumors, but athletes rarely take steroids in liquid suspension form. Users almost uniformly opt for the injectable or topical alternatives, which have chemical structures that aren't noxious to the liver. And as Yesalis observes, even oral steroids aren't causally linked to cancer; instead, some evidence associates them with benign liver tumors. . . .

Another commonly held belief is that steroid use causes aggressive or enraged behavior. Consider the case of San Francisco Giants outfielder Barry Bonds, whose impressive late-career home run hitting and built-up physique have long raised observers' eyebrows. [In 2002], Bonds, long known for being irascible, had a dugout shoving match with teammate Jeff Kent. A few columnists, including Bill Lankhof of the *Toronto Sun* and Jacob Longan of the *Stillwater News-Press*, obliquely diagnosed "'roid rage" from afar. "There's very inconsistent data on whether 'roid rage even exists," says Yesalis. "I'm more open to the possibility than I used to be, but its incidence is rare, and the studies that concluded it does exist largely haven't accounted for underlying factors or the placebo effect.". . .

Fears about steroid use also include other cancers, heart enlargement, increased blood pressure, elevated cholesterol levels, and musculoskeletal injuries. Upon closer examination, these too turn out to be overblown. Reports associating heart enlargement, or cardiomegaly, with steroid use often ignore the role of natural, non-threatening enlargement brought on by prolonged physical exertion, not to mention the effects of alcohol abuse. The relationship is unclear at best. Evidence supporting a link between steroids and ligament and tendon damage is weak, since steroid-related injuries are virtually indistinguishable from those occurring normally. And blood pressure problems, according to Yesalis, have been exaggerated. There is some associative evidence that steroid use can increase the risk of prostate cancer, but this link has yet to be borne out in a laboratory setting. No studies of any kind link the use of anabolics to testicular cancer. . . .

One reason the health effects of steroids are so uncertain is a dearth of research. In the almost 65 years that anabolic steroids have been in our midst, there has not been a single epidemiological study of the effects of long-term use. Instead, Yesalis explains, concerns about extended usage are extrapolated from what's known about short-term effects. The problem is that those short-term research projects are often case studies, which Yesalis calls the "lowest life form of scientific studies." Case studies often draw conclusions from a single test subject and are especially prone to correlative errors.

"We've had thousands upon thousands [of long-term studies] done on tobacco, cocaine, you name it," Yesalis complains. "But for as much as you see and hear about anabolic steroids, they haven't even taken that step.". . .

Problems Stemming from Prohibition

Criminalization of steroids [under the 1990 Anabolic Steroids Control Act] created dangers more serious than any that had prompted the ban. Once steroids became contraband, many athletes bought black-market anabolics that, unbeknownst to them, were spiked or cut with other drugs or intended solely for veterinary use. Physicians were forbidden to prescribe steroids for promoting muscle growth and thus were not able to provide steroid users with responsible, professionally informed oversight. New league policies even ban the use of steroids for recovery from injuries.

Combine the lack of medical supervision with the mind-set of the garden-variety steroid user, and you have a potentially perilous situation. "Many of those using anabolic steroids," says Penn State's Yesalis, "have the attitude that if one [dose] works, then five or 10 will work even better. That's dangerous."

A Government War on Steroids?

Does the sale of over-the-counter steroid supplements constitute a societal emergency requiring intervention by the Feds? No. "Where is the societal damage?" asked supplement company Syntrax Innovations' founder Derek Cornelius in *The Washington Post*. "[Critics] would have a point if people were having bad side effects, if people were dying in hospitals, but it's not happening. It's like making an issue out of something that's not.". . .

On the evidence marshaled so far by supplement critics, the bottom line is that we don't need to open a new anti-steroid front in an already highly destructive and failing War on Drugs.

Ronald Bailey, "On Steroids?" *Reason Online*, December 6, 2002.

Athletes who acquire steroids on the black market are loath to consult with their physician after they begin using regularly. If they do disclose their habit and ask for guidance, the physician, for fear of professional discipline or even criminal charges, may refuse to continue seeing the patient. For professional athletes, another deterrent to proper use is that all responsible doctors keep rigorously accurate records of their dealings with patients. The fear that those records might be leaked or even subpoenaed makes pro athletes even less likely to seek medical guidance.

Since many of the observed side effects of steroids—anecdotal, apocryphal, or otherwise—most likely result from excessive or improper use of the drug, one wonders: Can steroids be used for muscle building with a reasonable degree of safety? "The candid answer is yes, but with caveats," says [Rick] Collins, [an] attorney who specializes in steroid law. "It would need to be under the strict direction of a physician and administered only after a thorough physical examination, and it would need to be taken at reasonable and responsible dosages.". . .

Collins is quick to add that adolescents, whose bodies are already steeped in hormones, cannot use steroids safely. But the fact remains that the illegality of steroids makes responsible professional oversight virtually impossible.

Another puzzling distinction is the one made between steroids and other training supplements. Many baseball players have openly used androstenedione, a muscle-building compound that major league baseball hasn't banned even though it's merely a molecular puddle-jump from anabolic steroids. Androstenedione is a chemical precursor that is converted to testosterone by the liver. Creatine monohydrate, another effective supplement, is far more widely used than androstenedione and is virtually free of stigma. Creatine is chemically unrelated to anabolic steroids or androstenedione and also differs in that it does not manipulate hormone levels; rather, creatine allows muscle cells to recover from fatigue more quickly. But all three substances— creatine, androstenedione, and anabolic steroids—increase a naturally occurring substance in the body to promote the building of muscle tissue. Anabolic steroids simply accomplish this end more quickly and dramatically.

The list of "artificial" enhancements doesn't stop there. Indeed, the boundaries of what constitutes a "natural" modern athlete are increasingly arbitrary. Pitchers benefit from computer modeling of their throwing motions. Medical and pharmacological technologies help players to prevent and recover from injuries better than ever before. Even laboratory-engineered protein shakes, nutrition bars, and vitamin C tablets should theoretically violate notions of "natural" training. Yet no one claims these tools are tarnishing the competitive integrity of the game.

Muscle Beach Zombies

Rangers pitcher Kenny Rogers has said, in a bizarre admission, that he doesn't throw as hard as he can because he fears that the line drives hit by today's players, if properly placed, could kill him on the mound. And you need not read the sports pages for long to find someone complaining that today's "juiced" ballplayers are toppling the game's sacrosanct records by the shadiest of means. This sentiment began percolating when Roger Maris' single-season home run record tottered and fell to Mark McGwire in 1998. Since the Caminiti and Canseco stories broke, sportswriters have been resorting to preposterous rhetorical flourishes in dismissing the accomplishments of the modern hitter. Bill Conlin of the *Philadelphia Daily News*, for example, writes: "To all the freaks, geeks and 'roid zombies who have turned major league baseball into a Muscle Beach version of the Medellin Cartel: Take your records and get lost."

Yet baseball statistics have never existed in a vacuum. Babe Ruth became the sport's chief pantheon dweller without ever competing against a dark-skinned ballplayer. Chuck Klein of the Philadelphia Phillies posted some eye-popping numbers in the 1930s, but he did it in an era when runs were scored in bundles, and he took outrageous advantage of the Baker-Bowl's right field fence, which was a mere 280 feet from home plate. Detroit pitcher Hal Newhouser won two most valuable player awards and a plaque in Cooperstown in part by dominating competition that had been thinned out by World War II's conscription. Sandy Koufax crafted his run of success in the '60s with the help of a swollen strike zone. Also a boon to Koufax was the helpfully designed Dodger Stadium, which included, according to many, an illegally heightened mound. Gaylord Perry succored his Hall of Fame career by often calling upon an illegal spitball pitch. Take any baseball statistic, and something is either inflating or depressing it to some degree.

Beginning in the mid-'90s in the American League and the late '90s in the National League, home runs reached unseen levels. This fact has encouraged much of the present steroids conjecture. But correlation does not imply causation, as the deductive reasoning platitude goes, and there are more likely explanations for the recent increase in homers.

Home runs are up, in large part, because several hitter-friendly ballparks have opened in recent years. Coors Field, home of the Colorado Rockies since 1995, is the greatest run-scoring environment in major league history. Until the 2000 season, the Houston Astros played in the Astrodome, a cavernous, run-suppressing monstrosity with remarkably poor visuals for hitters. They replaced it with Enron Field (now renamed Minute Maid Park), which is second only to Coors Field in terms of helping hitters and boasts a left field line that's so short it's in violation of major league rules. The Pittsburgh Pirates, Milwaukee Brewers, and Texas Rangers also have recently replaced their old ballparks with stadiums far more accommodating to hitters. The Arizona Diamondbacks came into being in 1998; they too play in a park that significantly inflates offensive statistics. The St. Louis Cardinals, Baltimore Orioles, and Chicago White Sox have all moved in their outfield fences in the last few years. Add to all that the contemporary strike zone, which plainly benefits hitters, and it's little wonder that home runs are at heretofore unimaginable levels.

And then there is Barry Bonds and the momentous season he had in 2001. In the midst of Bonds' siege on McGwire's still freshly minted single-season home run record, Bob Klapisch of the Bergen County, New Jersey, *Record* made a transparent observation-cum-accusation by writing, "No one has directly accused Bonds of cheating—whether it be a corked bat or steroids. . . ."

Bonds is plainly bigger than he was early in his career. That fact, considered in tandem with his almost unimaginable statistical achievements, has led many to doubt the purity of his training habits. But Bonds had bulked up to his current size by the late '90s, and from then until 2001 his home run totals were in line with his previous yearly levels. So there's obviously a disconnect between his body size and his home runs. [In 2002] bulky as ever, Bonds hit "only" 46 homers, which isn't out of step with his pre-2001 performance. More than likely, Bonds had an aberrant season in 2001—not unlike Roger Maris in 1961.

Steroids vs. the Perfect Swing

This is not to suggest that no ballplayers are taking advantage of modern pharmacology. Rick Collins says he knows some major league ballplayers are using steroids but can't hazard a guess as to how many. And Yesalis believes that at least 30 percent of major league ballplayers are on steroids. . . .

If players are on steroids, how much of a difference is it making?

Not much of one, according to Chris Yeager, human performance specialist, private hitting instructor, and longtime weightlifter. . . .

"Upper body strength doesn't increase bat speed," he explains, "and bat speed is vital to hitting home runs. The upper body is used in a ballistic manner. It contributes very little in terms of power generation." Yeager likens the arms, in the context of a hitter's swing, to the bat itself: simply a means to transfer energy. A batter's pectoral muscles, says Yeager, "are even less useful."

Yeager isn't saying steroid use couldn't increase a batter's power. He's saying most ballplayers don't train properly. "There's a difference between training for strength and training for power," he says, "and most baseball players train for strength." If hitters carefully and specifically trained their legs and hips to deliver sudden blasts of power, then steroids could be useful to them, but by and large that's not what they do. "Mark McGwire hit 49 home runs as a 23-year-old rookie," Yeager says. "And, while I think he probably used steroids at some point in his career, he hit home runs primarily because of his excellent technique, his knowledge of the strike zone, and the length of his arms. Barry Bonds could be on steroids, but his power comes from the fact that he has the closest thing to a perfect swing that I've ever seen."

Much Ado About Nothing

In what at first blush seems counterintuitive, Yeager asserts that steroid use may have decreased home run levels in certain instances. Specifically, he points to Canseco. "I'm almost positive Canseco used steroids, and I think it hurt his career," says Yeager. "He became an overmuscled, one-dimensional player who couldn't stay healthy. Without steroids, he might have hit 600, 700 home runs in his career."

In short, steroids are a significant threat to neither the health of the players nor the health of the game. Yet the country has returned to panic mode, with both private and public authorities declaring war on tissue-building drugs.

The chief instrument in that war is random drug testing, which major league baseball adopted in September 2002 with the ratification of the most recent collective bargaining agreement. Players can be tested for drugs at any time, for any reason whatsoever. Leaving aside what this implies for players' privacy, testing is easily skirted by users who know what they're doing.

Sprinter Ben Johnson tested positive for steroids at the 1988 Summer Olympics and forfeited his gold medal, but subsequent investigation revealed that he'd passed 19 drug tests prior to failing the final one at the Seoul games. Yesalis says most professional athletes who use steroids know how to pass a drug test. Whether by using masking agents, undetectable proxies like human growth hormone, or water-based testosterone, they can avoid a positive reading. At the higher levels of sports, Yesalis believes, drug testing is done mostly "for public relations." Image protection is a sensible goal for any business, but no one should be deluded into thinking it eliminates drug use. . . .

Meanwhile, baseball's new collective bargaining agreement has firmly established drug testing in the sport. The Major League Baseball Players Association, contrary to what some expected, agreed to the testing program with little resistance.

The measure won't do much to prevent the use of performance-enhancing drugs in baseball, but it may serve as a palliative for the media. At least until the next cause celebre comes along.

"Leagues must ban players' use of even legal performance-enhancing substances . . . as well as of illegal counterparts like steroids."

Performance-Enhancing Drugs Should Be Banned from Professional Sports

Paul Weiler

Paul Weiler is the author of *Leveling the Playing Field: How the Law Can Make Sports Better for Fans*, from which the following viewpoint is excerpted. In it, he argues that performance-enhancing drugs, both legal and illegal, should be banned from the Olympics and from professional sports leagues. While the health effects of some of these substances are not fully understood, he writes, it is clear that the use of amphetamines, steroids, human growth hormones, and other drugs and supplements poses serious health risks. Weiler maintains that athletes most harmed by performance-enhancing drugs are those who would prefer to compete without using drugs but feel they must do so to keep up with the competition.

As you read, consider the following questions:

1. What performance-enhancing substance did Mark McGwire admit to using in 1998?
2. In Weiler's opinion, what is the "second-best option" for dealing with performance-enhancing drugs in sports?
3. What professional sports league's drug testing policy does the author compliment?

Paul Weiler, *Leveling the Playing Field: How the Law Can Make Sports Better for Fans*. Cambridge, MA: Harvard University Press, 2000. Copyright © 2000 by the President and Fellows of Harvard College. All rights reserved. Reproduced by permission.

The biggest reason for the resurgence of interest in baseball in the late 1990s was the phenomenal number of home runs being hit. Fans became most "homer happy" in 1998 as they watched Mark McGwire competing with Sammy Sosa to see who would replace Roger Maris as our home run record-holder. McGwire ended up breaking Maris's record of 61 home runs with 70 that season.

Everyone knows how close Sosa came to McGwire in 1998 (with 66 homers) and how close both came again in 1999 (with 65 and 63, respectively). What few fans realize, though, is that neither McGwire nor Sosa came close to breaking Babe Ruth's *true* home run record. Suppose we were to do the same kind of adjustment for home run inflation that we regularly do for economic inflation, for example, to calculate the real rise of the Dow Jones Index from the 1920s to the 1990s. In order for a McGwire or a Sosa (or Ken Griffey Jr.) to break Ruth's *real* home run record from the 1920s, he now has to hit more than 150, not just 60, home runs over the season. Put those figures together with the fact that Ruth was a pitcher of Hall-of-Fame quality for the Red Sox when they won their last World Series in Fenway Park back in 1918, before their owner, Harry Frazee, sold Ruth to the Yankees. It should now be clear why Babe Ruth was our greatest athlete in any sport in the past century.

A number of factors have contributed to the surge in home run hitting over the last several decades. One is the change in the design and quality, of balls and bats, the same as has happened to the balls and clubs or racquets in golf and tennis. Another is the size and shape of new ballparks, which have not only more luxurious seats but also walls that are easier to reach. In addition, the umpires have altered the strike zone to force pitchers to put the ball in a spot where it is easier to hit it a long way. Finally, the bodies of hitters are dramatically different than they were back in the 1920s.

There are a host of reasons why athletes are now in so much better shape. For our purposes here, the issue is whether such additional body strength (and speed or endurance) has been created by a kind of drug not targeted by the war on drugs—the performance-enhancer. The latest such substances to appear on the scene were Androstenedione ("Andro") and Creatine. It was the news of McGwire's use of Andro in 1998, along with use by other players such as José Canseco and Jeff Bagwell, that made thin a best-selling pill for youngsters wanting to follow that same path to glory. While the athletic pioneer with Creatine was Brady Anderson, who used it to turn himself into a 50–home run lead-off hitter, even more famous Creatine users have been Sammy Sosa, John Elway, who quarterbacked the Denver Broncos to Super Bowl Championships in 1998 and 1999, and Michael Johnson, the record-setting track and field star of the 1990s.

In late 1999 baseball authorities were still considering whether to make the use of Andro a sports offense (and no one was suggesting doing anything about Creatine). At least with Andro, the NFL has adopted a very different position, consistent with football's change of focus when Paul Tagliabue was installed as commissioner in 1990. Following the trail blazed by the International Olympic Committee [IOC] beginning at the 1972 Olympics in Munich, the NFL is now targeting its drug control efforts as much at performance-enhancing drugs like steroids (or Andro) as at mind-altering drugs like cocaine. That same priority was displayed in the original drug control program proposed to the NCAA [National Collegiate Athletic Association] in 1985 triggered by the scandal of steroid use by many American athletes at the 1983 Pan-American Games in Caracas, Venezuela. At the NCAA's January 1986 convention, marijuana and cocaine were added only as an afterthought to the testing and banning of steroids and amphetamines.

Health Effects

A decade earlier the *Washington Post*'s series "Drugs and Sports" had also focused principally on amphetamines, making only casual references to athletes' use of marijuana or cocaine. Amphetamines were colloquially known as "speed" because of their acceleration of the body's circulatory and respiratory systems. While they had a number of accepted medical uses, including as diet pills, these tablets had also become a common way to fight the fatigue felt by college students studying all night before their final exams, by truck drivers on long-distance hauls, or, in sports, by cyclists and marathon runners. In the NFL amphetamines were used to pump up players' aggressive instincts, especially among linemen, for whom control and rhythm were not as important as they were for quarterbacks. But even though amphetamines enhanced athletic performance in the short run, they created a significant risk of harm in the longer run. For example, their "speed-up" of the heart and liver occasionally resulted in cardiac convulsions or coma.

Keep Sports Drug Free

I say it does matter whether pro sports are clean or drug dirty. Here's why:

- You'll never know what's real or fake if you suspect a big percentage of players is on the juice. Spectator sports are built on the belief that the games aren't rigged. Otherwise, switch the dial to pro wrestling.

- The pro drug plague leaches down to high school and college players. Coaches say that's already happening. You think a 180-pound kid lineman won't be tempted to try the same chemicals as Joe Superstar?

- Athletes who think they're immortal are playing Russian roulette with their health by toying with drugs. Experts warn of heart disease and tumors. Ask the friends of former NFL stud Lyle Alzado, who blamed his death from cancer at 43 on steroids.

- Baseball especially is built on nostalgia, sentiment, past greatness. If 21st century homers are propelled by steroids, it makes a mockery of Babe Ruth, who trained on beer and hot dogs. The careers of Joe DiMaggio, Ted Williams and Mickey Mantle may be laughed away by modern sports junkies.

Sandy Grady, "Just Say Yes to Pro Sports Drugs?" *USA Today*, December 2, 2003.

By the 1980s the performance-enhancing drugs of choice for athletes were anabolic steroids, intended to make their bodies both stronger and faster. Steroids are a synthetic substitute for the male hormone testosterone. The synthetic form was designed to provide more of the muscle-building (anabolic) effect of testosterone while minimizing its masculinizing (androgenic) effect. Steroids were first developed as a mode of treatment for certain diseases, but the principal market for them soon was made up of athletes such as weightlifters, shotputters, and football players.

As a high school football player in the late 1960s, Lyle Alzado was too undersized to get a college athletic scholarship. But when he discovered the magic of steroids—his favorite was Dianabol—Alzado became an All-Pro defensive lineman who led the Denver Broncos to a Super Bowl appearance in 1977 and the Los Angeles Raiders to a Super Bowl victory in 1982. Later, in a 1991 *Sports Illustrated* cover story revisiting the problem of drugs in sports, Alzado depicted himself as a stark example of why athletes should *not* use steroids: he was dying of lymphomatic cancer of the brain.

The Alzado story was a dramatic example of the athletic advantages of steroids, but not a particularly accurate portrayal of their dangers. It is scientifically improbable that the type of cancer afflicting Alzado was the product of steroids. Indeed, one of the challenges posed by steroids, as well as their successors of the 1990s, human growth hormone (HGH) and erythropoietin (EPO), is that while sharply altering the body chemistry is likely to create some serious health risks, it is difficult to document precisely what and how serious those risks are. Making such determinations requires epidemiological studies that follow matched groups of users and nonusers of steroids, HGH, or EPO for two to three decades. This is the research procedure that led to the discovery of the dangers of another "miracle" substance— asbestos. Unfortunately, by the time the truth about asbestos was known and safeguards adopted in the 1960s, millions of American workers had already been exposed to the substance on the job, and hundreds of thousands were fated to die as a result. Not until the 1990s was it scientifically established that steroids can lead to conditions such as heart disease and liver cancer.

What about Andro and Creatine? Creatine is an amino acid powder, and Andro is a testosterone-producing pill; both enhance weight, strength, and muscular ability. Both Andro and Creatine are categorized as legal "dietary supplements" under the federal Food and Drug Act, which was significantly relaxed in 1994: this was some time after anabolic steroids had been classed as "controlled substances," illegal to use without a medical prescription. Athletes' use of Andro has been prohibited by Olympic and college sports authorities, as well as by the NFL, but not yet by any other professional team sport. Because of the physiological nature of this substance's effects, it will be another decade or two before epidemiological studies can document whether Andro poses risks to the body similar to those of steroids and amphetamines.

The Win-at-All-Costs Mentality

On the other side of that athletic coin is the immediate performance-enhancing value of steroids, amphetamines, HGH, EPO, and now Andro and Creatine. After the news broke in 1998 about the boost that Creatine had apparently given Elway during the Broncos' Super Bowl chase, and the one that Andro had given McGwire in his quest for the home-run record, over-the-counter sales of those substances soared, especially sales to high school athletes. The Andro phenomenon is an eerie reminder of the steroid revelations that surfaced at the 1988 Olympic Games in Seoul, with the rise and fall of Ben Johnson. In the early 1980s this Canadian sprinter was good but not great. Then he began using steroids to accelerate his training, and by 1988 he not only had beaten America's Carl Lewis in the 100-meter Olympic finals but had run what is still the fastest-ever time of 9.79 seconds. And awaiting victory by Johnson at the Olympics were more than $10 million in endorsement deals.

Two days later Johnson tested positive for steroids and lost it all—gold medal, record, and $10 million endorsement bonus. But he had already demonstrated to athletes around the world that such a substance could transform a middle-level runner into the world's fastest human being, at least as long as he could conceal his use of the drug. Of course, exposure to such a drug cannot be "hidden" from the body, and it may eventually reveal itself in a life-threatening disease. However, unlike workers exposed to asbestos at a naval shipyard or a construction site, many athletes feel that the "pot of gold" for winning in their sport is large enough to justify betting that they will not be the ones to suffer from those health hazards. A 1995 poll of aspiring Olympians found more than half saying that they were prepared to accept *dying* from a performance-enhancing drug in five years, if it would guarantee their winning a gold medal now.

The Harms of Performance-Enhancing Drugs

Because of the inherent interdependence of participants in sports, sports authorities should impose much tougher constraints on athletes' use of steroids than on their use of cocaine. Both cocaine and steroids do generate some risk of physical harm or death; and by contrast with the use of loaded guns, for example, their immediate physical impact is felt by those who choose to use them, not by other people. The intoxicating or addicting features of recreational drugs may still justify broad legal prohibitions designed to protect occasional drug abusers from inflicting harm on themselves, and thus on their families and society. However, reflecting on the Ben Johnson case reveals that performance-enhancing drugs like steroids actually impose much of their harm on *other* athletes who would prefer not to use the drugs.

When Johnson used steroids to dramatically improve his speed and performance at the 1988 Olympics, he also inflicted significant harm on the health and well-being of his present and future competitors. The same was true of the Irish swimmer Michelle Smith when she used HGH (and Andro) to allow her to surprise everyone by winning not one but three gold medals at the 1996 Olympics: Johnson's rivals such as Carl Lewis and Smith's rivals such as Janet Evans faced a Prisoner's Dilemma: either concede the Olympic golds to Johnson and Smith, or put their own lives and limbs at risk by using the substances themselves. After all, world-class athletes devote their lives to a sport in order to become champions, not just graceful losers. If use of performance-enhancing drugs becomes widespread, no one gets any special advantage from them. In that case, everyone is left worse off because of toxic exposure whose harmful consequences are likely to appear only after these athletes have left sports and the public eye.

One special characteristic of sports is the need to preserve whole-hearted competition among teams for the benefit of fans. That is why leagues must have and enforce rules barring players from throwing games or shaving points. Less obvious, but also crucial, are rules designed to create *fair* competition; in particular, to protect athletes against the pressure to sacrifice too much to win. Pursuit of this objective led Paul Tagliabue, after he became football commissioner in 1990, to establish in the NFL the first anti-steroid policy in professional sports.

But it is not enough for a sports authority simply to put on its books a rule that prohibits use of a substance like steroids. Effective enforcement of that rule is essential. Otherwise, when the governing body announces its ban on performance-enhancing drugs, most athletes will comply voluntarily, expecting their competitors to be doing so as well. But if enforcement is lax, a few athletes are likely to get away with breaking the rule and thereby beating their rivals on the field. So if we cannot achieve the ideal—effective control of unscrupulous rule-breakers—the second-best option may be to repeal the rule entirely, fully inform competitors of the risks of steroid use, and let the athletes decide whether or not to take their chances.

The Need for Systematic Drug Testing

In my view, systematic drug testing of all athletes is the best option. It was this IOC procedure that uncovered Ben Johnson's breaking of the rules and thus cost him his dramatic victory at Seoul. The most graphic illustration in the 1990s involved Chinese swimmers. After the Chinese team hired an East German coach in the mid-1980s, its swimming performance suddenly blossomed: China garnered a substantial number of gold medals at the 1988 and 1992 Olympic Games, and 12 of the 16 golds at the 1994 World Championship in Rome. But only a few months later, tests administered without warning to the Chinese team at the Asian Games in Hiroshima disclosed a host of drug users: by 1998, 27 of the team's top swimmers had been banned from international competition. That nation will have to reclaim its position in this sport by complying with, rather than violating, these key rules of the game.

However, the principal value of performance-enhancing drugs like steroids (unlike that of amphetamines) is realized in off-season training cycles. If the athlete ceases using steroids for a sufficient period before competing—something

Ben Johnson failed to do before Seoul—the drugs (but not the benefits) will disappear from the athlete's system before testing at the event. To address this problem, the IOC and other international sports authorities have expanded their programs to have the tester suddenly appear unannounced at the athlete's door to administer the test. It was this procedure that revealed Michelle Smith's use of HGH and Andro in the middle of the 1998 winter in Ireland, after she had tested negative during the 1996 summer games in Atlanta. Recognizing that same need for a safe and level playing field in football, the NFL Players Association has agreed that its members be subject to random testing for steroids and the like even during the off-season.

The steroids debate provides yet another illustration of what is special about sports, and of why the NFL and the NCAA have made the right judgments on this score. Leagues must ban players' use even of legal performance-enhancing substances like Andro, as well as of illegal counterparts like steroids. Players who use these substances create a significant risk not just for themselves but also for their competitors and successors, who face strong pressures to follow that same path in order to excel in their sport. And random year-round drug testing must accompany the ban to ensure that no players can get away with violating those rules.

Accepting the wisdom of this policy is one thing: implementing it is another, rife with difficult issues. Any testing process will make an occasional mistake with a false positive finding, and thus players must have a meaningful procedure for challenging and correcting such results. Since I cannot explore such operational questions in any detail here, I will simply note and compliment the carefully tailored procedural design that the NFL players and owners have worked into their Policy on Anabolic Steroids and Related Substances. Needless to say, the rather authoritarian policymaking processes of the NCAA and the IOC have performed less impressively on this score. The fact that professional athletes have organized into a union gives them not only the leverage to defend their personal interests but also the potential to devise win-win solutions with the owners to problems facing their sport.

"All kinds of performance-enhancing methods should be allowed in professional sports."

Performance-Enhancing Drugs Should Not Be Banned from Professional Sports

Claudio M. Tamburrini

Claudio M. Tamburrini is a senior researcher in the department of philosophy at Gothenburg University in Sweden. In the following viewpoint he argues that "doping"—the use of performance-enhancing drugs by athletes—should be allowed in professional sports. Tamburrini maintains that while fitness, enjoyment, and fun are the goals of amateur athletes, professional athletes are paid to win. He believes it is unethical for such athletes to be prohibited from using substances that can help them do their job better, even if such substances are harmful to the athlete's health. Moreover, he believes that lifting the ban on doping would help athletes by allowing them to openly consult with a physician about which substances they use.

As you read, consider the following questions:
1. Into what three groups does the author divide performance-enhancing drugs?
2. How does the author respond to the argument that legalizing doping would put pressure on all athletes to use drugs?
3. What types of performance-enhancing drugs does the author believe young professional athletes should be permitted to use?

Professionalism and widespread sponsorship brought about for athletes the prospect of getting considerable rewards for their efforts. This, no doubt, puts them under great temptations. Illicit short cuts to victory, though obviously not providing excellence in a sport discipline, might nonetheless secure economic benefits as well as fame and respect, at least as long as the unfair strategy for victory is not uncovered.

Doping is one of those short cuts. To many people, this indicates that the current development that elite sport is undergoing is unsound.

But, what is doping? The term is used to cover different things, with varying effects on the individual's health. When discussing forbidden performance-enhancing methods, it is useful to make the distinction between doping substances and doping techniques.

Among the former group (doping substances) we have those that are:

1. *harmful though legal*, when prescribed by a physician. Within this group, we find anabolic steroids, growth hormones, beta-blockers, ephedrine, stimulants of the central nervous system such as amphetamines, etc. At present, there is no doubt that prolonged and uncontrolled (that is, without medical supervision) use of these substances yields serious health damages. However, the state of our knowledge concerning the effects of their short-term and properly dosed administration is still deficient.

2. *harmful and strictly illegal* (for instance, central stimulants such as cocaine).

3. both *harmless and legal*, such as diuretics and caffeine. These substances are generally used and there are practically no restrictions on their use, other than those imposed on athletes by the International Olympic Committee (IOC).

Among banned performance-enhancing techniques, perhaps the most known is blood-doping. It consists in the withdrawal, storing and re-injection of the athlete's own blood to increase oxygen intake. Although the method—when properly administered—involves no known health risks, it is proscribed by some world sport associations. A similar effect is obtained by altitude training. This latter method, however, is not forbidden by doping regulations.

Benefits of Lifting the Ban

Now before this discussion on doping takes off, it could be asked why we need to scrutinise the rationale behind doping bans. Isn't the use of performance-enhancing techniques obviously wrong? In spite of this widespread intuition, actually there are some arguments that support lifting current bans.

First, the prohibition on doping puts arbitrary restraints on the further development of sports. Athletes are thus impeded from perfecting the skills specific to their discipline.

Furthermore, the ban is responsible for our present lack of knowledge on the eventual harmful effects of doping. This is highly relevant, as doping, in spite of the ban, occurs and will continue to occur. Lifting the prohibition would then allow us to conduct research aimed at reducing harm provoked by actual unsupervised doping use.

Finally, doping also deprives professional elite sport from the transparency it so badly needs at present. We know for sure that Ben Johnson and Diego Maradona doped. But we can only suspect that the late Florence Griffith-Joyner also did it. Who hasn't sometimes felt that his admiration for a sport hero was darkened by the doubt whether the victor really was 'clean'? In elite sports, we may have arrived at a situation in which we often celebrate not the most excellent, but the most sly athlete, the one who dopes and gets away with it. The significance of this lack of transparency for the educational role of sports cannot be exaggerated.

In spite of all these reasons, the ban on doping apparently has wide support among athletes, sport officials and the public. It thus seems reasonable to ask, What's wrong with doping?

Different reasons are advanced to support the ban. A first reason is that doping is damaging for athletes' health. . . .

Now, even if the present objection were tenable, why should we care? After all, we generally accept risks involved in different sport practices. Too intensive training causes physical injuries, and the lethal figures for certain sports (for instance, climbing and boxing) are clearly higher than the number of doping victims. . . .

As commonly stated, the present objection to free doping is paternalistic: the ban on doping is justified in order to secure the wellbeing of sport practitioners. Thus, sportsmen are impeded from practising their activity, in the way they judge more appropriate. Professional athletes are not allowed to decide for themselves what risks they are disposed to confront in the pursuit of their careers. . . .

Professional athletes are no doubt unwise if they ruin their health (through doping or through other training techniques) in order to win. But, in that case, other professional categories are no wiser. We do not see this as a particularly disturbing situation from a moral point of view; it is generally accepted that people should be granted the right to make unwise decisions. Why should professional athletes be denied that right? . . .

The Coercion Argument

Prohibitionists also affirm that doping does not simply harm the individual athlete. In their view, the ban is justified because doping is harmful to others. To begin with, they contend that doped athletes coerce reluctant colleagues into doping. Otherwise, they will not be able to reach the same competitive level as those who dope. Second, athletes (especially successful ones) are social models to the young. There is then a risk that young people will try to emulate their sport heroes and go for doping, or even for a drug culture. Finally, there is the criticism that underlines the impossibility of restraining doping to professional, adult sportsmen: if allowed, doping will probably be adopted even by amateurs and junior top athletes. Will these objections suffice to support the ban?

Due to the situation of hard competition that characterises professional sports, would it be fair to say that doped athletes put their more reluctant colleagues under pressure to dope themselves?

In my opinion, to speak of coercion in this context is an overstatement. Athletes reluctant to dope will, no doubt, be put under a pressure to emulate their less prudent colleagues. But nothing hinders them from still refusing to dope. They will not, then, be among the reduced group of habitual winners. This, however, is not morally problematic. In competitive activities, not everyone can win. In the realm of professional ethics, it is widely accepted that benefits should be distributed in relation to efforts and risks undertaken. An ambitious war correspondent puts her life at risk to obtain interesting news or the most impressive picture. If she succeeds, she will be rewarded. By so doing, she is, albeit indirectly, challenging her colleagues to do the same, if they want to achieve a similar success. Should we prohibit war correspondents from coming too near the battle line, to avoid submitting other war correspondents to such a pressure? The suggestion seems to me preposterous. Every well-informed adult has a right to decide by herself which risks to take in the exercise of her professional activity, so long as this does not harm others. Athletes should not be treated differently.

My conclusion is that, other things being equal, if an athlete risks her health to attain victory, while others are more prudent, it is only fair that the victory goes to the former. . . .

Athletes as Social Models

A common objection to allowing doping in sport competitions is that sports stars are social models for young people. Thus, without the ban, athletes will probably be emulated in their doping habits by young people, and this might lead to increases in both drug consumption and doping use among the young. Considerable social harm will follow from that. The . . . objection assumes that performance-enhancing methods (including doping substances) can be placed on an equal footing with recreational drugs. This, however, is a misunderstanding (though a very common one). It is simply wrong to connect doping and drugs in the way these objectors suggest. Whatever the sacrifices an athlete makes in order to achieve a high level of performance, she will be jeopardising her chances to win if she takes drugs. In that sense, with or without doping, sports still are incompatible with drugs. This is, in my opinion, the correct interpretation of the common saying that 'Sport should be "clean"'. Sport is obviously incompatible with unhealthy life: if you want to engage in physical activity (on a professional *or* amateur basis), you need to adopt a moderate way of living. That is quite other thing from abstaining from doping. Properly administered, doping might even be required to achieve a high level of performance. It is unwarranted to assume that the public, even young people, will be unable to see this fact, or that the misunderstanding cannot be taken care of by means of proper information.

The Futility of Steroid Testing

Passing [a steroid test] can mean . . .

- The athlete doesn't use steroids.
- He uses steroids daily but with a masking agent.
- He uses steroids, but all traces are flushed out of his system within two or three days.
- He uses a steroid recipe fashioned by a designer famous for undetectable potions.
- He used steroids as training aids two years ago, bulked up, kept buff with madman workouts and now needs a juice refill only every January.
- He uses human growth hormone, or insulin-like growth factor I. These replicate steroid enhancement, but no test exists for them.

Dave Kindred, "It Doesn't Take a Genius to Pass a Steroid Test," *Sporting News*, August 19, 2002.

The struggle against illegal drugs is a justified cause. So is the goal of restricting smoking and drinking among the young and the population in general. It is questionable, however, whether athletes should be used as a weapon in that struggle. Athletes should certainly not be curtailed in their professional freedom, no matter how commendable the goals we are trying to achieve in the process—at least, no more than people in other professions are. . . .

Finally, we have no reason either to assume that a ban on doping would be the most effective way of reducing its use among young athletes. Open dialogue and communication between coaches, parents and young sports practitioners might turn out to be a better way to come to terms with doping abuse by the young. . . .

Teenage Professional Athletes

Up till now, I have been advocating free doping in the realm of professional sports. My stance could be criticised by pointing to the fact that in some highly competitive professional sports (tennis, for instance) many athletic stars today are teenagers. Should they also be allowed to dope? Does my proposal include them as well?

Yes and no. Minors should not be allowed to indulge in practices that might jeopardise their health. Using dangerous doping substances, such as many of those included in types 1 and 2, is no doubt one of these practices. This sort of constraint is reasonable, as teenagers usually lack the maturity to have complete awareness of the risks these decisions might entail. Nor should parents and legal guardians be allowed to decide such matters on behalf of young people. Greedy adults might, after all, be tempted to put the health of their children at risk in order to get material benefits. This constraint is also in accordance with current social and legal practices.

But, with relation to harmless doping methods we also should be liberal in relation to young athletes. My previous arguments, then, apply to them as well. This comprises, it should be noted, all doping methods included in type 3, but it might also include some of the substances listed in types 1 and 2. Though dangerous, we should not exclude the possibility that, in the future, we might learn to neutralise the noxious effects of these substances, at least when they are properly administered. As long as their use cannot be expected to hinder harmonic growth, it should be left to young top athletes to decide whether to use them or not. Otherwise, they would be competing with adult practitioners in unequal conditions. . . .

The Nature of Sports

A common objection to performance-enhancing methods is that doping runs counter to the nature of sports competitions. According to a widely accepted notion, within the framework of current regulations, a sports contest consists in establishing as objectively as possible the inequalities between athletes that are relevant for the sports discipline. Athletes differ in skills, training motivation, sacrifices made, etc. Fairness requires that all athletes abide by the same rules, and that the outcome of the competition will be settled exclusively by those differences. These restrictions are expected to contribute to the uncertainty of the outcome, which—in its turn—is said to give the activity the excitement that captivates sports audiences. Doping, on this line of reasoning, deprives sports of its excitement, as it makes the outcome of the contest more predictable. The contest, rather than being a challenge between persons, is then transformed into a struggle between bodies, supported by different technological devices. . . .

This argument has been advanced by Robert Simon in the following terms:

> The whole point of athletic competition is to test the athletic ability of persons, not the way bodies react to drugs. In the latter case, it is not the athlete who is responsible for the gain. Enhanced performance does not result from the qualities of the athlete qua person, such as dedication, motivation, or courage. It does not result from innate or developed ability, of which it is the point of competition to test. Rather, it results from an external factor, the ability of one's body to efficiently utilise a drug, a factor which has only a contingent and fortuitous relationship to athletic ability.

The conclusion Simon arrives at is that '. . . the use of performance-enhancing drugs should be prohibited in the name of the value of respect for persons itself'.

Now, what is first needed is a more nuanced account of what doping actually is. Doping is no magic pill that makes dedication, goal-oriented training, motivation and effort completely superfluous. Doping stands for small marginal differences in athletic performance. That means that all the personal attributes in which the winner has to excel in order to get the victory will still be needed in sport contests, with or without performance-enhancing methods.

Simon is well aware of this fact, however, but he does not consider this point as decisive. He says that even 'if all athletes used drugs, they might not react to them equally'. This makes him insist that, in that case, 'outcomes would be determined not by the relevant qualities of the athletes themselves but rather by the natural capacity of their bodies to react to the drug of choice'.

Simon's criterion, however, is problematic; at least, if consequently applied, it would equally condemn standard training techniques. The capacity to profit from a particular diet or training method is also an innate 'capacity of the body'. He has a straightforward answer to this: 'Capacity to bene-fit from training techniques seem part of what makes one a superior athlete in a way that capacity to benefit from a drug does not'. Thus, Simon manages to condemn doping and save standard training by refusing to apply his criterion in a consistent manner. He simply stipulates his assertion, but gives no reason for it. His move therefore strikes me as question-begging. . . .

Lift the Ban

In this [viewpoint], the traditional arguments against doping have been submitted to scrutiny. I could summarise my con-clusion by saying that the ban on performance-enhancing methods constrains the professional activities of athletes, and that the reasons often advanced to support that constraint do not stand criticism. The prohibition rests either on arbitrary delimitations or on ungrounded prejudices, or both.

But, it could then be asked, why does it enjoy so much support amongst the general public? In my opinion, differ-ent reasons could be advanced to account for such support.

One reason could be that the public still associates doping with a drug-liberal society. This is a misconception. I have already argued for the plausibility of being restrictive on recreational drugs, while at the same time advocating lifting the ban on doping. The amount of aggregated social harm originated by these two practices will probably differ.

From the assertion that 'sport has to be clean', another usual misconception consists in concluding that doping is against the 'nature' of sport. At least in one sense of the term 'clean', the above standpoint no doubt expresses a valuable insight. Whether we practise sport as a leisure activity or as a profession, our lifestyle should be a healthy one. Alcohol and drug intake are counterproductive to any kind of sport activity, no matter how intense it is. From this, however, it does not follow that doping also is incompatible with any kind of sport practices. To grasp this argument properly, we need to concentrate on the distinction (still unobserved by some people, and unduly neglected by most) between recreational and professional sports. This leads us into the next reason lying (in my opinion) behind public support for the ban on doping.

The primary goal of recreational sports is to promote health and enjoyment for its practitioners. To dope within such a context will no doubt be counterproductive. The athlete who dopes will probably ruin her health and will not experience any amusement. Professional sport, instead, is ruled by different goals. A professional athlete aims to become excellent in her discipline and to achieve the external goals—mainly prestige and money—that usually follow such victory. Given the hard competition that characterises professional sports, doping is not only rational, but even necessary, for securing those goals. Although they have a common origin, recreational and professional sports have evolved in different ways and today constitute two very distinct social practices. And different social practices should reasonably be guided by different rules.

Professional sport, then, goes free from the accusation of promoting unsound strategies to victory. If my arguments in this chapter are correct, all kinds of performance-enhancing methods should be allowed in professional sports. Certain doping damages will then be unavoidable. This is a regrettable effect of my proposal. These damages, however, are not essentially different from the injuries that affect other professional categories. We should do everything we can to minimise them, as we do in other professions, short of implementing paternalistic restraints in the activity, A condition for reducing doping injuries, I have argued, is lifting the ban. But we will not be able to prevent all doping injuries fully. We should not be surprised. Working always breaks down workers' health, so why should sports jobs be different?

Periodical Bibliography

The following articles have been selected to supplement the diverse views presented in this chapter.

Hal Bodley	"Union Has Power, Duty to Rid Game of Steroids," *USA Today*, March 19, 2004.
Richard Glen Boire	"Dangerous Lessons," *Humanist*, November/December 2002.
Richard Corliss	"Baseball Takes a Hit," *Time*, March 15, 2004.
Jeff Greenfield	"Can the Government Clean Up the Game?" *Sports Illustrated*, March 15, 2004.
Jeffrey Kluger	"The Steroid Detective," *Time*, March 1, 2004.
Jere Longman and Marjorie Connelly	"Americans Suspect Steroid Use in Sports Is Common, Poll Finds," *New York Times*, December 16, 2003.
Richard Sandomir	"As Games Begin, Talk of Steroids Dominates," *New York Times*, March 3, 2004.
Mark Sappenfield	"How Far Sports Steroid Scandal Might Spread," *Christian Science Monitor*, February 19, 2004.
Sports Illustrated	"Unnatural Selection," May 14, 2001.
Mark Starr	"The Dope on Doping: Making the Case Against Performance-Enhancing Drugs," *Newsweek*, February 23, 2004.
Michael Stroh	"Future Jocks," *Science World*, September 27, 2002.
Tom Verducci	"Is Baseball in the Asterisk Era?" *Sports Illustrated*, March 15, 2004.

For Further Discussion

Chapter 1

1. Between the first two viewpoints in the chapter, whose depiction of youth sports most closely matches your own experience? Explain your answer.

2. Do you agree with John R. Gerdy's contention that organized sports are inappropriate for children below the age of thirteen? Why or why not?

3. After reading the viewpoints by John Hoberman and Richard E. Lapchick, do you feel that participation in sports benefits black youth? Explain your answer.

4. Are there any professional athletes that you feel are good role models? Did the viewpoints by Mark Patinkin and Ashley Brown change your opinion of whether athletes should be role models, and if so, how?

Chapter 2

1. On the issue of whether college athletes should be paid, whose viewpoint did you find more persuasive—D. Stanley Eitzen's or Jason Whitlock's—and why?

2. Robert M. Sellers, Tabbye M. Chavous, and Tony N. Brown contend that college entrance requirements affect black student-athletes disproportionately. After reading the viewpoint, do you feel that academic standards are inherently unfair if they affect student-athletes from different racial groups differently? Explain your answer.

3. After reading the viewpoints by William S. Saum and Danny Sheridan, what, if any, effects do you think that a nationwide ban on college sports wagering would have?

Chapter 3

1. After reading the viewpoints by the *New York Amsterdam News*, Roger Clegg, and Greg Franke, which author do you feel provides the most persuasive evidence? Explain your answer.

2. After reading the viewpoints by the Women's Sports Foundation and Jessica Gavora, do you feel that Title IX is a beneficial law? Why or why not?

Chapter 4

1. Tom Verducci asserts that steroid use is rampant in Major League Baseball while Dayn Perry maintains that the media has exaggerated the problem. Which viewpoint do you find more persuasive, and why?

2. Do you feel that performance-enhancing drugs have any place in sports? Did the viewpoints by Paul Weiler and Claudio M. Tamburrini affect your opinion? Explain your answers.

Organizations to Contact

The editors have compiled the following list of organizations concerned with the issues debated in this book. The descriptions are derived from materials provided by the organizations. All have publications or information available for interested readers. The list was compiled on the date of publication of the present volume; the information provided here may change. Be aware that many organizations take several weeks or longer to respond to inquiries, so allow as much time as possible.

American Association for Health, Physical Education, Recreation, and Dance (AAHPERD)
1900 Association Dr., Reston, VA 20191-1598
(703) 476-3400
Web site: www.aahperd.org

AAHPERD is the largest organization of professionals supporting and assisting those involved in physical education, leisure, fitness, dance, health promotion, and education and all specialties related to achieving a healthy lifestyle. The organization works to provide members with an array of resources, support, and programs to help practitioners improve their skills and so further the health and well-being of the American public. It has several publications, including the *American Journal of Health Education*, the *Journal of Physical Education, Recreation, and Dance*, and the *Research Quarterly for Exercise and Sport*.

Canadian Centre for Ethics in Sport (CCES)
202-2197 Riverside Dr., Ottawa, ON K1H 7X3 Canada
(613) 521-3340
Web site: www.cces.ca

CCES's mission is to promote ethical conduct in all aspects of sport in Canada. It achieves this mission through research, promotion, and education relevant to ethics in sport, including fair play and drug-free sport. CCES also administers Canada's domestic drug-free sport program. It publishes information about drug testing in Canada as well as discussion papers, including *Know Now: Ethical Discussion Paper on Self-Testing for Drug-Use* and *2002–2003: A Landmark Year in Ethical Sport*.

Canadian Interuniversity Sport
801 King Edward, Suite N205, Ottawa, ON K1N 6N5 Canada
(613) 562-5670
Web site: www.cis.ca

The Canadian Interuniversity Sport is the national governing body of university sport in Canada. It is composed of the majority of degree-granting universities in the country. Its Web site provides the latest scores, scheduling, and information on sports of all member universities as well as athlete media coverage and coaching assistance.

Center for the Study of Sports in Society
360 Huntingdon Ave., Suite 161 CP, Boston, MA 02115-5000
(617) 373-4025
Web site: www.sportinsociety.org

The center's philosophy is that sports are a reflection of society with all of its good points as well as its negative ones. It works to reform sports for the better through programs that teach student-athletes important life skills. It publishes a quarterly newsletter for each of its various programs.

Institute for Diversity and Ethics in Sport
University of Central Florida (UCF)
400 Central Florida Blvd., Orlando, FL 32816
Web site: www.bus.ucf.edu

The institute is part of the UCF College of Business Administration's DeVos Sport Business Management Graduate Program. This program focuses on the business skills necessary for the sports industry. The Institute for Diversity and Ethics in Sport serves as a comprehensive resource for issues related to gender and race in amateur, collegiate, and professional sports. It researches and publishes the *Racial and Gender Report Card*, an annual report on hiring practices in coaching and sport management, student-athlete graduation rates, and racial attitudes in sports.

National Alliance for Youth Sports (NAYS)
2050 Vista Pkwy., West Palm Beach, FL 33411
(561) 684-1141
Web site: www.nays.org

The alliance is a leading advocate for positive and safe sports and activities for children. NAYS coordinates a Time Out program to help communities evaluate their sports programs and a Start Smart! program to help children get involved in sports. NAYS also promotes a set of standards and recommendations for parents, coaches, and officials, which are available on the NAYS Web site.

National Coalition Against Violent Athletes (NCAVA)
PO Box 620453, Littleton, CO 80162
Web site: www.ncava.org

The coalition was formed in 1997 in response to the growing number of violent crimes committed by athletes in all areas of the sports world. It believes that athletes should be held to the same standards and laws as the rest of society, and it works to educate the public on this issue. The NCAVA Web site provides statistics and news updates on violence among athletes as well as articles on violence prevention.

National Collegiate Athletic Association (NCAA)
700 W. Washington St., PO Box 6222, Indianapolis, IN
46206-6222
(317) 917-6222
Web site: www.ncaa.org

The NCAA is the administrative body that oversees intercollegiate athletic programs. It opposes betting on college sports and supports academic standards for high school students applying for athletic scholarships. The NCAA publishes information on student-athlete graduation rates, academic standards, sports betting, NCAA rules and regulations, and a variety of other topics.

National Council of Youth Sports (NCYS)
7185 SE Seagate Ln., Stuart, FL 34997
(772) 781-1452
Web site: www.ncys.org

NCYS is a nonprofit organization representing the youth sports industry whose mission is to advance the values of participation and educate and develop leaders. The council is composed of over 150 youth sports organizations. It publishes the *Youth Sports Today* newsletter six times annually as well as the 2001 *Report on Trends and Participation in Organized Youth Sports.*

Positive Coaching Alliance (PCA)
Department of Athletics
Stanford University, Stanford, CA 94305-6150
(866) 725-0024
Web site: www.positivecoach.org

PCA's goal is to transform the culture of youth sports to give all young athletes the opportunity for a positive, character-building experience. The alliance believes that winning is a goal in youth sports but that there is a second, more important goal of using sports to teach life lessons through positive coaching. PCA offers the National Youth Sports Awards to coaches and organizations that help achieve this goal. PCA also publishes a quarterly newsletter.

President's Council on Physical Fitness and Sports (PCPFS)
Dept. W, 200 Independence Ave. SW, Room 738-H,
Washington, DC 20201-0004
(202) 690-9000
Web site: www.fitness.gov

PCPFS serves as a catalyst to promote, encourage, and motivate Americans of all ages to become physically active and participate in sports. Assisted by elements of the U.S. Public Health Service, the council advises the president and the secretary of Health and Human Services on how to encourage more Americans to be physically fit and active. PCPFS publishes fact sheets, statistics, and a quarterly research digest on sports and fitness.

Women's Sports Foundation (WSF)
Eisenhower Park, East Meadow, NY 11554
(800) 227-3988
Web site: www.womenssportsfoundation.org

The foundation is a charitable educational organization dedicated to advancing the lives of girls and women through sports and physical activity. It supports stronger enforcement of Title IX of the Educational Amendments of 1972, and helps educate the public by providing facts, statistics, and background data on sports-related issues for women and girls. WSF publishes a newsletter as well as reports and position papers on issues involving sports and gender.

Bibliography of Books

David L. Andrews, ed.   *Michael Jordan, Inc.: Corporate Sport, Media Culture, and Late Modern America.* Albany: State University of New York Press, 2001.

Jeff Benedict   *Public Heroes, Private Felons: Athletes and Crimes Against Women.* Boston: Northeastern University Press, 1997.

Richard O. Davies   *America's Obsession: Sports and Society Since 1945.* New York: Harcourt Brace College, 1994.

Richard O. Davies and Richard G. Abram   *Betting the Line: Sports Wagering in American Life.* Columbus: Ohio State University Press, 2001.

Robert Elias, ed.   *Baseball and the American Dream: Race, Class, Gender, and the National Pastime.* Armonk, NY: M.E. Sharpe, 2001.

Jon Entine   *Taboo: Why Black Athletes Dominate Sports and Why We're Afraid to Talk About It.* New York: Public Affairs, 2000.

Jessica Gavora   *Tilting the Playing Field: School, Sports, Sex, and Title IX.* San Francisco: Encounter Books, 2002.

John R. Gerdy   *Sports: The All-American Addiction.* Jackson: University of Mississippi Press, 2002.

John Hoberman   *Darwin's Athletes: How Sport Has Damaged Black America and Preserved the Myth of Race.* Boston: Houghton-Mifflin, 1997.

Richard E. Lapchick   *Smashing Barriers: Race and Sport in the New Millennium.* Lanham, MD: Madison Books, 2001.

Andy Miah   *Genetically Modified Athletes: The Ethical Implications of Genetic Technologies in Sport.* New York: Routledge, 2004.

Shane Murphy   *The Cheers and the Tears: A Healthy Alternative to the Dark Side of Youth Sports Today.* San Francisco: Jossey-Bass, 1999.

Mariah Burton Nelson   *The Stronger Women Get, the More Men Love Football: Sexism and the American Culture of Sports.* New York: Harcourt Brace, 1994.

Dennis Perrin   *American Fan: Sports Mania and the Culture That Feeds It.* New York: Avon, 2000.

Douglas T. Putnam   *Controversies of the Sports World.* Westport, CT: Greenwood Press, 1999.

James Quirk and
Rodney Fort

Hard Ball: The Abuse of Power in Pro Team Sports.
Princeton, NJ: Princeton University Press,
1999.

James L. Shulman and
William G. Bowen

*The Game of Life: College Sports and Educational
Values.* Princeton, NJ: Princeton University
Press, 2001.

Lissa Smith, ed.

Nike Is a Goddess: The History of Women's Sports.
New York: Atlantic Monthly Press, 1998.

Murray Sperber

*Beer and Circus: How Big-Time College Sports Is
Crippling Undergraduate Education.* New York:
Henry Holt, 2000.

Allen L. Stack and
Ellen J. Staurowsky

*College Athletes for Hire: The Evolution and Legacy
of the NCAA's Amateur Myth.* Westport, CT:
Praeger, 1998.

Paul Weiler

*Leveling the Playing Field: How the Law Can
Make Sports Better for Fans.* Cambridge, MA:
Harvard University Press, 2000.

Index

advertising, 58
African Americans
  are disproportionately excluded from college athletics, 71–72
  are overrepresented in sports, 70
  athletic identity of, 31–32
  college athletic eligibility requirements are unfair to, 73, 74–76
    con, 81–82
  racial folklore on differences between whites and, 35–37
  standardized tests and, 79
  see also black youth; coaches, minority
Alomar, Roberto, 48
Alzado, Lyle, 160
American Association of University Women (AAUW), 123, 129
American Gaming Association, 94
American Institute for Research (AIR), 73
amphetamines, 158–59
anabolic steroids. *See* steroid use
Anderson, Brady, 158
Andrews, James, 144
Androstenedione (Andro), 157–58, 160–61
athletes
  cannot be viewed as role models, 51–53
  in outreach programs, 42–43
  poor examples set by, 48
  see also college athletes
athletic directors, 117
athletic scholarships
  academic requirements for, 71
  African Americans on, 70
  undermine higher education, 67
  for women, 115

Bagwell, Jeff, 158
Bailey, Ronald, 150
baseball, surge in home run hitting in, 157
black youth
  academic/intellectual pursuits of, 33, 37–38
  balance of academic and athletic goals by, 42–43
  benefits of playing sports for, 43–44
  career aspirations of, vs. white youth, 35
  overemphasis on sports and athletes by, 32–35

should be encouraged to play sports, 44
  unrealistic athletic aspirations of, 42
blood-doping, 166–67
Bonds, Barry, 143, 148, 153
Boston, Massachusetts, 41, 46
Boston College football team, 88
Boston Youth Sports Needs Assessment Survey, 41
Bowen, William G., 22
Bowl Championship Series (BCS), 58
Brentwood Academy v. Tennessee Secondary School Athletic Association, 119
Brooks, David, 24
Brown, Ashley, 50
Brown, Tony N., 69
Brown University, 124
Bryant, Kobe, 51

Caminiti, Ken, 136–37, 142, 146
Canseco, Jose, 138, 146, 154, 158
Chavous, Tabbye M., 69
children's sports
  adults ruin, 18
  adults should not dominate, 21–23
  benefits of, 12, 16
  cutting programs in schools for, 40
  de-organized, 19–21
  difference between adult-run and children-run, 18–19
  disadvantages of, 13, 16
  fun in, 19
  girls benefit from, 44–45
  hard work emphasized in, 28–29
  help build character, 25–26
  learning about failure and responsibility in, 28
  need for investing in, 40–41
  parental influence and, 16
  parental wariness of, 41–42
  personal development through, 27
  positive role modeling by athletes in, 48
  pressures from adults in, 20
  providing more resources for, 45–46
  surveys on, 41
  team loyalty and, 29
  team playing in, 26–28
Clarett, Maurice, 56
Clark, Nicolas, 20
Clegg, Roger, 104
Clemens, Roger, 48
coaches
  financial benefits for college, 59,